Praise f[...]

Oh, my, a book on the pastorate that is about, well, pastoring, shepherding! It's a rare breed in our ambitious and managerial age. But it's a biblical breed who know that the minister is, from first to last, a minister of God's grace. I have said this about few books in my long life, but it clearly applies to this one: required reading for every pastor, a book destined to become a classic.

> —MARK GALLI
> Senior managing editor
> *Christianity Today*

"Wisdom doesn't have the blurts" writes Lee Eclov, but rather listens with questions and then frames an answer with the grace of Christ. Eclov follows his advice in *Pastoral Graces*, a poignant and engaging book that composes a beautiful vision of pastoral ministry. Having grown in wisdom for over three decades in pastoral ministry, Eclov weaves warm stories together with biblical truth for the benefit of his readers. And if we as pastors are to survive the long marathon of pastoral ministry, we need the careful wisdom of books like *Pastoral Graces*, a cool and refreshing cup of grace for thirsty pastors.

> —CHRIS BRAUNS
> Pastor of The Red Brick Church,
> Stillman Valley, Illinois

Lee Eclov has a heart, a pastor's heart, and he can put into inspiring and cashmere-sweater words its movements. Reading this book is like talking to Lee at his best. If you are a pastor, this book will most likely leave you with renewed feelings about the joy and privilege of being not the executive of a corporation but rather the shepherd of the flock.

—CRAIG BRIAN LARSON
Editor of PreachingToday.com

Lee Eclov is the kind of pastor I want to have as my pastor. He is the sort of pastor I would like to be. This book draws back the veil to reveal the remarkable and mysterious way that God works through ordinary shepherds. If you are a pastor, read it. It will make you grateful for the privilege. If you have a pastor, it will make you thankful that God has given your church such a gift.

—JOHN KOESSLER
Chairman of Pastoral Studies Department,
Moody Bible Institute

Plenty of books teach ministers how to be CEOs. Some texts teach them how to be good preachers. Only a few inculcate valid principles for pastoring, and rarer still are those that do it well. *Pastoral Graces* is a gem of a book that does it superbly.

—CRAIG BLOMBERG
Distinguished Professor of New Testament,
Denver Seminary

At its core, pastoral leadership connects the divine to the lives of all those around us through the demonstration of God's abundant grace. From Lee's life as a pastor, he explains how God uses pastors to be dispensers of God's grace. Pastors will appreciate Lee's practical suggestions on how to make grace the center of our leadership.

—CRAIG WILLIFORD
President, Trinity International University

PASTORAL

GRACES

PASTORAL
GRACES

REFLECTIONS ON THE
CARE OF SOULS

LEE ECLOV

MOODY PUBLISHERS
CHICAGO

© 2012 by
LEE ECLOV

All rights reserved. No part of this book may be reproduced in any form without permission in writing from the publisher, except in the case of brief quotations embodied in critical articles or reviews.

All Scripture quotations, unless otherwise indicated, are taken from *the Holy Bible, New International Version®*, NIV 1984®. Copyright ©1973, 1978, 1984 by Biblica, Inc.™ Used by permission of Zondervan. All rights reserved worldwide.

Scripture quotations marked NIV are taken from the *Holy Bible, New International Version®*. NIV®. Copyright © 2011 by Biblica, Inc.™ Used by permission of Zondervan. All rights reserved worldwide.

Scripture quotations marked KJV are tken from the King James Version.

Edited by Brandon O'Brien
Interior design: Ragont Design
Cover design: Left Coast Design
Cover image: Getty Images / Photographer Emmanuelle Purdon
              Collection: Photodisc / Credit Emmanuelle Purdon
Author photo: Magen Davis

Library of Congress Cataloging-in-Publication Data

Eclov, Lee.
    Pastoral graces : reflections on the care of souls / Lee Eclov.
    p. cm.
    ISBN 978-0-8024-0567-8
    1. Pastoral care. 2. Pastoral theology. 3. Pastoral counseling.
    4. Church work. 5. Grace (Theology) I. Title.
    BV4011.3.E28 2012
    253'.2—dc23

                                            2012003881

We hope you enjoy this book from Moody Publishers. Our goal is to provide high-quality, thought-provoking books and products that connect truth to your real needs and challenges. For more information on other books and products written and produced from a biblical perspective, go to www.moodypublishers.com or write to:

Moody Publishers
820 N. LaSalle Boulevard
Chicago, IL 60610

1 3 5 7 9 10 8 6 4 2

Printed in the United States of America

For Susan,
who loves me and loves being a pastor's wife;
and for Anders, my son,
with whom I am well pleased.

CONTENTS

Introduction   11

1. *Un*called, Then the Hand in My Back   17
2. Authority, Wisdom, and Grace. Especially Grace   31
3. Public Grace   47
4. Public Grace Refreshed   59
5. Portable Grace   73
6. Decorating with Grace   87
7. Building with Broken People   99
8. March into the Smoke   115
9. "I'd Have Waited All Night"   131
10. "Lead Me Gently Home"   145
11. "Safe thus Far"   159

Notes   173
Acknowledgments   175

INTRODUCTION

DOCTORS ENTER the practice of medicine. Lawyers, the practice of law. Pastors enter the practice of grace. Grace is our stock-in-trade. But practicing grace is not much like the professions of medicine or law.

First off, God's grace—being grace—starts giving before we even know how badly we need it. God starts saving us before we know we're drowning. Then, when we realize we must cry for help, our salvation through Christ comes loaded with far more benefits than we fathom. "You do not lack any grace-gift," says Paul in 1 Corinthians 1:7. We spend the rest of our days discovering how rich we are, none of our blessings deserved or earned.

This life of grace comes with responsibilities for grace. Like Christ, our pioneer in grace, we are born again not to be served, but to serve, and to serve redemptively through Christ. God's grace not only washes us, it outfits us with Jesus' basin and towel.

Pastors, like all believers, are agents of grace. But we dispense the grace of Christ as no other believers do. We are shepherds. Search as we might for a word more suited to our contemporary culture, *shepherd* is the only word that will do. If we hope to understand what we've been called by God to do, we have to step into a foreign world of sheep and pastures, folds and staffs, night watches and wilderness searches. Look hard at the timeless figures "keeping watch over their flocks by night." Patient, long-suffering, committed to the often lonely routines of care. That's how God wants us to see ourselves. In fact, that is one way God sees Himself.

No one is born with the aptitude for being one of the Lord's shepherds. No one starts planning a career thinking, *I guess I'll go into the practice of grace.* But when we are called, God gives us a miraculous instinct for the work. We commonly call it "a shepherd's heart." While I suppose that some pastors have personalities that give them a leg up, no one has the makings of a shepherd apart from God's grace. You think you're headed for a career in business or education, a trade or an art, and the next thing you know, you're standing in some pasture with a shepherd's crook in your hand, surrounded by sheep. It's a career comedown, unless you know about grace.

An old TV show, *The Greatest American Hero,* introduced a young school teacher who discovered he had superpowers he couldn't quite get used to. The opening sequence each week showed a guy pulling a kind of red Superman suit out of a suitcase with a wary, what's-going-on-here look on his face. The next thing you see is him in his suit flying headlong into a wall, then making a flailing crash landing onto rocks. When he finally does fly off the edge of a building, he wobbles precariously.

Learning to pastor is a lot like that. Pastoral grace is a kind of superpower God gives us, and at first we don't quite know what to do with it. We put it on, perhaps in a service where older, stronger believers than ourselves stand around us, their hands pressed on our shoulders, conferring a cape of grace. I don't know about you, but I didn't feel any different on my first official day as a pastor, except that a sense of responsibility and insecurity weighed heavily on me. Yet in the days and weeks that followed, I found myself dispensing the grace of Christ with an effect that was new to me, and something of a surprise. I had seen God's grace work before when I shared the gospel, taught Scripture, or counseled the young adults I worked with. But with this new role, I gradually realized God had given me a Christlike instinct for shepherding that was new to me. It was as though I had received a blood transfusion from the Good Shepherd. If you're a pastor, you probably know what I mean.

These strengths and responsibilities don't come upon any of us suddenly. We realize them gradually, even before anyone calls us Pastor. And none of us come by these instincts naturally. All we have and all we do as shepherds of God's flock—as pastors—are grace-gifts, spiritual instincts as foreign to our natures as flying. I still run into walls sometimes and wobble as though I've never done this before. But I am, by a miracle of God's grace, a shepherd.

In the books and conferences urged upon us as pastors and in the pastoral models put before us, we feel a kind of relentless pressure to be better strategic and visionary leaders, more compelling communicators, more astute theologians, and better culture-shaping evangelists. With good reason. Leadership, preaching, theology, and outreach are our work, and often our weaknesses. But all of these other assignments get in line behind Peter's instruction to us, "Be shepherds of God's flock that is under your care."

This book is intended to take some of the wobble out of our shepherding and to give us confidence in this supernatural instinct for grace that God conferred upon us when He gave us our shepherd's heart. In the chapters that follow, I will tell some of my stories and how they've helped me to understand this work God calls us to do. I'm confident my reflections and stories will resonate with other pastors and church leaders. When pastors get together, we always tell stories and our best stories tell how grace has worked itself out in our ministries.

First, our call. I know all Christians are called to serve Christ, often to particular places of service in the church and the world. But not many are called by God specifically to speak for him—to be what I call Wordworkers. In the following pages, we'll think about three special strengths God gives us as pastors to do just that: authority, wisdom, and grace. Then we'll look at what I call public graces—some of the ways pastors keep grace fresh on Sunday mornings—and portable graces—when we take our shepherd's work on the road to hospitals, funeral homes, and coffee shops.

Next, we'll look behind the scenes to the inward working of our churches. Grace should be every church's interior decorator. And grace always builds with the broken. Pastors better get used to that!

I'll also talk about God's grace to me when, like a Civil War general, I had to raise my hat on my sword so the troops could march with me into the smoke, wondering how many steps I had left. Also, no story about pastoral grace would be complete without reflecting on the ways God graces His shepherds through the precious people who follow us.

Finally, we will think about endings, because God's grace is always orienting His people toward home. One of the pastor's greatest privileges is making people homesick. I will reflect, too, about how we "finish the course," about the day promised to faithful elders "when the Chief Shepherd appears, [and] you will receive the crown of glory that will never fade away."

I suspect some pastors will read these stories and wonder why their ministries have been so much more difficult than mine. I have been blessed to serve churches who loved and cared for my family and me. That's the grace of God, pure and simple. But of course, I'm not telling you all the stories either.

Pastors are in the practice of grace for Jesus' sake. Since shepherding is a God-given assignment, it is too hard for us. How many times does a pastor think, *They never taught us this in seminary*? But God gives grace indiscriminately. Years ago I memorized 2 Corinthians 9:8. I have it framed on my wall. "And God is able to make all grace abound to you, so that in all things at all times, having all that you need, you will abound in every good work." All grace abound. This is the richest verse I know.

This book is called *Pastoral Graces* because the grace of God, in the work He gives His shepherds, takes many forms. None come without "Jesus Christ and him crucified." None are gifts we can rustle up on our own. None can be kept to ourselves. God makes all these graces abound to His pastors because He so dearly loves His flock.

Chapter One

*UN*CALLED, THEN THE HAND IN MY BACK

ONCE, I THOUGHT I'd make a good pastor.

I seemed born with a knack for it. I was only three when I told my first story from the church platform. Cute as a bug's ear, I was, sitting in my little red rocking chair with an oversized red book upside down in my hands. I chirped, "Mary and Joseph were on their way to Bethlehem." Right then the relatives started saying, "He looked like a little preacher up there!" It wasn't long before I was preaching from the high hassock in our living room.

In high school I started leading the once-a-month Sunday evening "singspiration" at Rose Hill, the country church in northeastern South Dakota that was my family's spiritual home. I mastered the song leader's smile on that platform, and how to pray like a preacher. Everyone could see I had a future in the church.

My main reason for going to our denominational school, Trinity College in Deerfield, Illinois, was to get on a traveling gospel team. Most Christian colleges had them in those days. Small musical ensembles made for good PR when you could get a church service together on almost any night of the week. The seven of us in our group, Heirborn, sang nearly every weekend in a church or two and toured for three summers. I got to know churches—church buildings, at least—inside and out. I made small talk with pastors, napped in the nurseries, and foraged food from secret stashes in youth room closets. I also came to love church people. I liked their stories of first steps and long walks with Jesus. This was also my first exposure to the fraternity of pastors. I began to think they were my kind of people.

But a double whammy waited.

As I headed into my senior year, I learned that a church in the area was looking for a part-time choir director and youth pastor. I called, had a short meeting with the pastor, and got the job on the spot. I learned to direct a cantata, how to plan a series of Bible lessons, and endured a camping trip to the boundary waters of northern Minnesota. I liked the twenty or thirty kids I worked with, but the majority of them were unchurched and I didn't know how to ride herd on all their shenanigans.

I had been there about a year when I arranged an appointment with the pastor. (We almost never had meetings.) I never got to my agenda because no sooner had I sat down than he told me, "I don't think this is working out." I caught my breath. It was a Friday morning and he said that Sunday would be my last day. He gave me some reasons—things we had never talked about before—and that was it. I never saw most of the kids in our group again. Thirty years later, when

I was invited to a big church anniversary event there, I told the lady who called that returning would be a bit awkward. "You know I was fired from your church, don't you?" I asked.

She was taken aback. "No one ever knew why you left," she said. "You were just gone."

Until then I had rarely failed at anything. That was partly because I didn't take chances, and partly because I was an overachiever. So for me this failure was a doozy.

CALLING UNRAVELED

I probably would have walked away from the ministry then and there, but I had registered for seminary and classes started only a week later. It was too late to change plans, so I plowed forward. But inside I was mortified. Thank God for that. Grace had a toehold.

The next spring, as my first year at Trinity Evangelical Divinity School drew to a close, a friend told me his home church back in our native South Dakota was looking for a summer intern. Rapid City is on the edge of the Black Hills, only a few miles from Mt. Rushmore, and it sounded like a grand adventure. A couple of letters back and forth, and things were set.

Under Pastor Stokka's gentle guidance, I began to learn what it was like to be a pastor. I led Bible studies, put church services together, and hung out with kids. Pastor Stokka and I talked about the ministry, and he took me with him to visit hospitals and homes—the part of the job that terrified me most. I counseled a few people and led someone to Christ. My confidence came back.

In the course of that summer internship, I was required to read a few books about being a pastor. One of them talked about the call to ministry. The message, loud and clear to this day, was, "If you can do anything other than be a pastor, do it." (I think every pastor I've ever mentioned that line to over the years has nodded in agreement.) Pastoring is good work, but it isn't exactly a career choice. I could easily see myself doing other things, and apparently that was a deal breaker. So there it was. God had not called me to the ministry. After all that. Go figure.

GOD SOMETIMES ENROLLS US IN HIS OWN KIND OF UNDERGROUND SEMINARY TO SCHOOL US IN GRACE BEFORE HE EVEN CLEARS HIS THROAT FOR A CALL.

That fall I eased out of seminary by taking just one class and starting a job raising funds for Trinity. No one glad-hands better than I do, so it seemed I had found my niche. I set a career goal of someday heading up that department.

Then I got a new boss. He was more disciplined and demanding than I was used to. My job review that spring didn't go well. Each of his six criticisms hit me like a body blow. I don't suppose I had ever heard so many of my failings in one place at one time. A month or two later, he dropped the hammer. "We'll pay you through the summer," he said—generously—"but June 10 will be your last day."

On that Friday afternoon in 1977 I walked out of my department alone, the last to leave. As I carried my box of stuff out to the car, I had trouble seeing through my tears. No party or cake. No one stayed to say thanks. No one said good-bye. If that wasn't bad enough, that night we were invited to the seminary graduation. It was my class, the guys I'd started with. They crossed the platform to get their MDiv degrees, most with pastorates or mission fields ahead of them, while I sat watching from the shadows with nothing.

I know now that God sometimes enrolls us in His own kind of underground seminary to school us in grace before He even clears His throat for a call.

My wife, Susan, and I were married in the middle of our senior year in college and we have always been involved in pastoral ministry together. We have both always loved it. In those early years we matured in Christ and in serving Him. I started a thriving young adults group and was elected to the Deacon Board. I had found my Christian calling as all believers do, using our spiritual gifts to build the Body of Christ. I was thankful for all God had invested in me to make me a useful layman.

CAPTIVE CAPTIVES

There is a short video clip in Ephesians 4. Picture an upward road, crowded with an unchained gang of captives, newly taken slaves who sing, "Free at last!" and "He has made me glad!" They delight to see out ahead of them their Conqueror

Christ. The Bible says, "When he ascended on high he took many captives." The captive church, including us, parades toward paradise.

But unnoticed by most of our brothers and sisters in their upward journey, Christ in his Emmaus disguise slips in and out among us. Here He taps someone on the shoulder and points to the side of the road. There He slips in behind others and whispers to them. Their puzzled look says, "Who? Me?" and He nods. Everyone on that highway was taken captive once by Christ, thank God, and now some are captured again. Captives twice over. Born again, again.

WE ARE THE GOSPEL TRADESMEN
WITH SWEAT-STAINED WORK SHIRTS, WELL-WORN
TOOL BELTS, ACHY KNEES, AND THE INSIDER'S
KNOWLEDGE OF HOW SOULS ARE BUILT.

What does Jesus do with these captive captives? He outfits them with the Word and gives them back to his upward-bound church as gifts. "When he ascended on high, he took many captives and gave gifts to his people. . . . So Christ himself gave the apostles, the prophets, the evangelists, the pastors and teachers, to equip his people for works of service, so that the body of Christ may be built up" (Ephesians 4:8, 11–12 NIV).

There is no earthly reason why the Lord pulled these particular captives out of the company of the heaven-bound and set the Word burning on our tongues. All our saintly siblings are gifted by Christ to serve one another in His Body as surely as we are, but we are among the Wordworkers. That is what I call the apostles, the prophets, the evangelists, the pastors and teachers. God divinely equips these particular believers to speak to the world and the church on His behalf. So far as I can tell, God did not single any of us out for this work because He liked our résumés or found us in a talent search. I suspect He chose us because, ever since creation, God finds special creative delight in making something from nothing, *ex nihilo*.

Christ's Wordworkers, these four ministry cousins, have different voices. Apostles have voices that can be heard over the din of a whole discordant culture, like a tornado warning siren. They step on unclaimed shores and proclaim a beachhead in the King's name. Prophets can bellow like town criers, stirring even the soundest sleepers with "This is what the Lord says." Evangelists sing with God's sweetest words, "Repent and believe the Good News. Jesus Christ died and rose again to save sinners. Come home! Come home!"

Then there are my people—the pastors and teachers. I think of pastors and teachers as the journeymen of Wordworking. We are the gospel tradesmen with sweat-stained work shirts, well-worn tool belts, achy knees, and the insider's knowledge of how souls are built.

PASTORAL GRACES

All these captives know, if they have their wits about them, that like a turtle on a fencepost, they didn't get where they are by themselves. In fact, to say that God called them seems like a tame way of describing what happened. Collared or captured is more like it. For me, when God's call came, everything else went gray.

FOUR TIMES IN FIVE DAYS I HEARD,
"YOU SHOULD BE A PASTOR."

During that wilderness summer of 1977, God schooled me in trust. Just as both the severance pay and summer ended, I was offered a position raising funds for a new Christian ministry, Living Bibles International, started by Kenneth Taylor, who had written *The Living Bible*. My assistant and I started from scratch, so it was a fascinating year of learning, administering, and traveling. But I had a growing sense of foreboding. Sooner or later, I would have to ask wealthy people, face to face, for big money. I would have to walk into executive offices or the homes of people the age of my grandparents and ask if they would contribute thousands of dollars to the cause of Bible translation. It was worthy work, but I knew I just didn't have the nerve. I had failed twice before and I was afraid it was going to happen again.

As part of my first annual review, my boss, Dr. Lars Dunberg, had me write about my gifts and goals. I don't remember what I wrote but I remember our meeting. It was a Monday afternoon in September and the first thing he said when I sat down was, "With your interests, why aren't you in the ministry?" He meant the pastorate. I hadn't seen that coming.

The next day a close friend, whose seminary graduation I'd watched on that dark June night, dropped in to see me. When he asked how the job was going I said, "I don't know how long I can do this. I'm afraid I'm not cut out for fundraising." Almost offhandedly he said, "Well, I've always thought you should be a pastor."

That evening when I got home, I told my wife Susan about our visit. We had been married almost five years at that point, and she had always said—only half-joking—that she never wanted to be married to a farmer or a pastor. So I was truly surprised when she said, "He's right. You should be a pastor."

On Friday morning of that same week, I got a phone call from a church in Colorado. They remembered me from when our college group, Heirborn, had sung there at least six years earlier. "We're looking for a youth pastor," the man said, "and you came to mind." I didn't pursue that position. But I didn't have to get my hearing checked either. Four times in five days I heard, "You should be a pastor."

There I was, minding my own business among the marching captives of Christ, when I felt a hand in the small of my back and a whisper, "Come with Me." Despite the obvious quiet ways God had been steering me, when His call came, it took me completely by surprise.

Two weeks later the associate pastor at the church we attended resigned. And just like that, the door opened. I was offered a position as assistant pastor. The church only required that I finish my seminary education part-time while working full-time. And they would pay for it!

On Sunday, December 10, 1978, under the clear call of God, I became a pastor—a real pastor—for the first time.

"THE SPIRIT OF THE SOVEREIGN LORD IS ON ME"

An African-American pastor friend invited me once to an ordination service for a couple of young men in his church. My wife and I had slipped into the back row of the crowded church when my friend tapped me on the shoulder. "Come with me," he said. "You'll be in the processional."

"The processional?" I asked. I had no idea what he was talking about. But a moment later pastors were marching down the aisle two by two. *What have I gotten myself into?* I wondered. I ended up in VIP seating to the side of the platform. I settled into the back row, caught my wife's grin, and figured I could lie low from then on.

Just then my host, who was sitting right in front of me, turned around in his chair and whispered over his shoulder, "You'll be reading the Scripture text. Isaiah 61:1–2."

"Ah, okay," I said, and thumbed my way to the passage that begins, "The Spirit of the sovereign Lord is on me." *Oh yes, that one,* I thought. *Just two verses. I can do that. It'll be over in a second.* Then I waited about an hour for my turn.

Finally, I climbed the platform steps to the old pulpit. I

opened my Bible and intoned, "The Spirit of the Sovereign Lord is on me."

The congregation stopped me dead in my tracks: "Amen! That's right! Amen!"

After I found my place again I forged on, ". . . because the Lord has anointed me to preach good news to the poor." I was feeling the love, so I punched the word preach a bit and there it came again:

"Preach the good news! Amen! Preach!"

I girded up my loins and marched boldly onward. "He has sent me to bind up the brokenhearted."

And it rolled back at me like an echo from heaven. "Bind UP!" "Praise God!" "Thank You, Jesus!"

"To proclaim FREEDOM for the captives."

Some laughed for the joy of it. Some clapped their hands.

"And release from DARKNESS for the prisoners."

Again, they ran out to meet the Word with palm branches and hosannas.

Two verses could take a long time to read. "To PRO-CLAIM the year of the Lord's FAVOR and the day of vengeance of our GOD."

"Yes!! Hallelujah!" Feet stomped on the wooden floor. Applause—applause!—for the greatness of the commission.

I closed my Bible and stood there amazed. And I wished like everything they'd given me more than two verses to read.

According to Luke 4, Jesus read those words to a wide-eyed gathering of the Sabbath faithful in Nazareth. Surely those ancient promises had never sounded so good. Then He rolled up the scroll and sat down. When no one said anything,

Jesus broke the pregnant silence, "Today this scripture is fulfilled in your hearing." Then Luke reports, "All spoke well of him and were amazed at the gracious words that came from his lips" (Luke 4:21, 22). The gracious words. Words of grace.

Isaiah gives us a fitting passage to read when a pastor is ordained, like the two young men that Sunday afternoon. Paul reminded Timothy, "Devote yourself to the public reading of Scripture, to preaching and to teaching." Wordwork, all of it. "Do not neglect your gift, which was given you through prophecy when the body of elders laid their hands on you" (1 Timothy 4:13–14 NIV). I don't quite understand all that happened there, but it is clear that God gave Timothy a gift in that holy moment that he didn't have before, and that his gift required bringing God's Word to God's people. I think Timothy's gift was the same as that commission given to Jesus, and that He keeps giving to those He calls as shepherds. "The Lord has anointed me [too] to proclaim good news to the poor. He has sent me [too] to bind up the brokenhearted, to proclaim freedom for the captives and release from darkness for the prisoners, to proclaim the year of the Lord's favor." Jesus first, and then His pastors.

Proclaiming grace always starts with the good news of redemption and resurrection. But grace has so much more to tell the redeemed. Gracious words, not always spoken aloud, cancel debts and bandage hearts. Gracious words open cell doors and tell people that their long dark wait has turned into the Lord's New Year's Day.

In Isaiah 61:3 NIV God continues, "to comfort all who mourn, and provide for those who grieve in Zion—to bestow on them a crown of beauty instead of ashes, the oil of joy instead of mourning, and a garment of praise instead of a spirit of despair. They will be called oaks of righteousness, a planting of the Lord for the display of his splendor."

I've loved that last line about the oaks of righteousness ever since one of the first couples I married asked to me to use it as a theme for their wedding. Their marriage endures oak-like to this day. The church I serve, the Village Church of Lincolnshire, is set amidst towering old oaks, so we've adopted that half verse as our motto. "They shall be called oaks of righteousness, a planting of the Lord for the display of his splendor."

A few years ago, on my tenth anniversary with this congregation, I asked for a new pulpit. It is beautifully crafted from oak by an expert woodworker who carved oak leaves and acorns into the border. Fitting, I think, for a pulpit and for the pastor called to the Wordwork of grace.

Chapter Two

AUTHORITY, WISDOM, AND GRACE. ESPECIALLY GRACE

A CARPENTER told me once that, in theory at least, he could build a house with three tools: a hammer, a saw, and a T-square. God has equipped us pastors in many wonderful ways, beginning with the message of the cross. But these three tools seem most indispensable for our work: authority, wisdom, and grace. And the greatest of these is grace.

AUTHORITY

I hadn't been a pastor more than a few weeks when I first felt the weight of pastoral authority. A woman probably fifteen years my senior had been harshly critical of another person. I had an unexpected divine appointment with her in the foyer, with no one else around, and I knew I needed to confront her. I don't remember the words I used anymore, but I know I approached her as a pastor. To my amazement, she listened to me. She slumped and said I was right and that she was sorry. I walked away sobered by the experience. I knew I had just had my first direct experience of pastoral authority. It felt weighty, too big for me.

God *authorizes* pastors. You usually hear the texts at pastoral installation and ordination services. "I *charge* you, in the sight of God and Christ Jesus and the elect angels, to keep these instructions without partiality" (1 Timothy 5:21). "I give you this charge: Preach the Word; be prepared in season and out of season; correct, rebuke and encourage—with great patience and careful instruction" (2 Timothy 4:1–2). "Be shepherds of God's flock that is under your care" (1 Peter 5:2). Charges like those change us.

In 2 Kings 2, just before Elijah was taken up in the chariot of fire, his protégé Elisha asked for a double portion of his spirit. The Bible says when Elijah was gone, Elisha tore his clothes. Then he picked up the cloak that Elijah left behind— the King James Version called it the mantle—and struck the water of the Jordan River with it. It was time to find out whether or not Elijah's spirit had been passed on to him. "Where now is the Lord, the God of Elijah?" he cried, and the water parted. I assume that, with his old garments shredded, Elisha always wore Elijah's cloak after that. It is like that when God endows pastors with spiritual authority.

It may come as a surprise, but God doesn't give pastors authority primarily so we can muscle through a new philosophy of worship or whip the missions committee into shape. We do have a certain authority to get things done around church, but I call that Authority the Lesser. It is conferred by our job description when we're hired. Authority the Greater is the mantle—the cloak—that God lays across our shoulders to empower our Wordwork.

I like authority as much as the next guy, but this *pastoral* authority is different. Let me count some ways.

Don't Speak for Yourself

Pastoral authority requires us always and only to serve our Master's wishes and words. We have a lot in common with the presidential press secretaries. They are expected to stand in front of an audience and speak for the president. They are to say what the president wants said and to explain as the president himself would. But press secretaries get in deep trouble if they say what the president never intended, if they try to make *their* words *his* words. So it is for pastors opening the Bible in sermons, Bible studies, or counseling. Do you ever get so used to speaking for the Lord that you think your own opinions are divinely inspired? There's a fine line there, but it is a dangerous thing to flash the badge of divine authority for personal use.

WE DON'T JUST TELL PEOPLE
WHAT GOD WANTS THEM TO DO.
WE ARE ALSO SPIRITUAL FIRST RESPONDERS.

Pastoral authority requires that we are straightforward with God's Word. Not unkind, or tactless, or unnecessarily blunt, but we must be direct. Someone praised me once for being bold in the pulpit. I felt sheepish. I don't usually find it difficult to be direct when I'm preaching. I don't consider it a virtue. What *is* hard is confronting someone personally. "Brother, I need to tell you something difficult: This ministry is not the right place for you. I'm going to have to ask you to step away from it." Or, "Friend, do you know how hurtful those words were? This has to stop." I have two suggestions, two spoonfuls of sugar to help the medicine go down. First, don't confront someone till you've gathered up love for them. It can take awhile, but if you don't consciously love the person you face, your words will inflict blunt force trauma. Secondly, smile whenever you can. Come kindly. A sympathetic smile says you aren't there to hurt them.

Step into the Mess

Pastoral authority is not all about laying down the law. When I think of a policeman's authority, I think first of his right to enforce the law—to break up parties, give official warnings, or arrest people. But his authority also means that he walks into trouble when the rest of us are heading for the exits. I don't suppose cops relish that risk, but it goes with the badge. Pastoral authority is like that. We don't just tell people what God wants them to do. We are also spiritual first responders. As one of my students put it, "We step into the mess."

No one was in the office but me when Monica called. She

was frantic because she couldn't reach her teenage son Luke, who was supposed to be home. He had been deeply despondent when she left that morning, and now he wasn't picking up his phone. She worked too far away to get there quickly and begged me to go to their place. "Can you please go over there? The back door is open," she said. She was afraid he had committed suicide.

I arrived about twenty minutes later and went around to the back. I was frightened at what I was about to find. "Luke," I called. "Luke, are you here?" I could hear the TV, but he wasn't in the living room and I turned it off. Dead quiet. "Luke. It's Pastor Lee. Your mom asked me to come to see if you're all right. Are you here?" Nothing. I looked up the staircase where I could see into the bathroom. There he was, sitting on the floor, head between his knees, perfectly still. I caught my breath. "Luke!" I got to the top of the steps and then he looked up at me.

"What's happening, man? Your mom is really worried about you. I'm going to call her." While we waited he told me about the girlfriend who left him and his frustrations with trying to get his high school equivalency diploma. Typical teenage angst; but for a boy with no father to give him emotional ballast, it was devastating. I listened and sympathized. I got in his face a little. I hugged him and prayed for him. In the days after, I called and texted. Our youth pastor called, too, but Luke never responded.

Sometimes when pastors step into a mess we pick up the wounds of others. Our eyes get a little sadder.

Paths of Righteousness

Pastoral authority requires that we lead God's flock on paths of righteousness. There are a lot of books and seminars for pastors about leadership. I've read some and they helped. We need to know how to lead a church toward the vision God has given us. We need to know how to lead through the upsets of change. Pastors identify with Joshua and Nehemiah, leading people to claim God's blessings and to build a holy city. Beyond that, shepherds lead people on solitary paths of illness, or painful waiting, and even through the valley of the shadow of death.

In all these pilgrimages, the pastor's task is not merely to get people from point A to point B. The Good Shepherd teaches us that we must guide them all the way "in paths of righteousness for his name's sake." I've learned to tell those who do not know which way to turn, "Today, if nothing else is clear, do not sin. Some kind of sin will seem like a relief or escape, but don't sin. It will only make things worse." I've learned, too, from watching heroic saints, to say, "God may not make this trial go away and He may not tell you why. But those who have been through the fire tell us to cling to the Lord, no matter what. He is faithful."

Authority without the Usual Perks

The authority God invests in pastors does not come with the usual perks of leadership. You don't really get to be the boss of anything. (That's the part that seems to get lost in some Christian leadership books.) People will ignore you just as they ignore God; yet *still* we're expected to lead them. Jesus tells us explicitly that we cannot lord it over others, but rather we must be their servants. *Foot washing* servants! It is a hard way to get things done. Plus sometimes God Himself practically kills us "so that [Jesus'] life may be revealed in our mortal bodies" (2 Corinthians 4:11).

WISDOM SITS DOWN NEXT TO US
AS WE LISTEN TO A PARISHIONER.
WISDOM LISTENS WITH QUESTIONS.

All in all, though, pastoral authority is a great gift to us and to God's flock. Scripture needs no help, of course. Yet God puts His Word in a pastor's heart and hands and something wonderful happens for the ill or hungry, the agitated or stubborn who listen and see. The shepherd's God-given authority amplifies what God has said. When good shepherds spread a table before the flock of God, it is God's Word on the plates, and our enemies can only watch from the shadows.

WISDOM

Wisdom, says Proverbs, is like an eloquent and elegant woman, a diligent and creative helpmate. Wisdom is lovely, gowned in grace.

The first thing wisdom will tell us, no matter what we're

facing, is to fear the Lord. Even the most dismal problem is God's throne room. Then she always points us straight to the cross of Christ and His empty tomb. She tells us that every solution or insight runs through the wisdom and power of Christ.

Wisdom Listens

Speaking wisely is not usually the same as giving advice. Most of us are sorely tempted to quick fixes, the pastoral version of "take two aspirin and call me in the morning." Wisdom, on the other hand, doesn't have the blurts. Wisdom sits down next to us as we listen to a parishioner. Wisdom listens with us until the part of the story hiding behind the door comes out, until the person before us knows they are loved, until the person's soul finally gets a word in edgewise. Wisdom listens with questions.

While we're listening, whether to someone we're counseling, a board discussion, or our small group's prayer requests, we're also listening for the Holy Spirit to speak. I imagine having one of those discreet earbuds, like the Secret Service wears. We're attentive to what's happening around us, but we're also listening intently to the murmured guidance of God in our inner ear. If we wait and don't talk so much, He will speak. If He doesn't, say to the person across from you, "I don't know what God wants us to think about this. Let's pray and ask Him." After that, wait. For a week, if you have to.

It isn't often that I feel God tell me directly what to say next, but when I listen for Him and trust Him to speak, interesting questions form in my mind and elusive connections come together. I begin to see the issue beneath the issue. Sometimes in those moments I see how Scripture reframes what I'm hearing. A story may come to mind or the name of someone in the church who would be a good helper. Sometimes wisdom just sympathizes.

OUR JOB IS TO HELP PEOPLE
REFRAME THEIR GRIEF THROUGH
THE COUNTERINTUITIVE WORD OF GOD.

Once in the pastor's group I treasure, one of the brothers told us how heavyhearted he was over a mother-daughter duo who was constantly coming to him for money and help. It had started with one of those phone calls looking for a handout and never stopped. They never came to church or showed any interest in the Lord. But the thing was, he cared about them and had helped them again and again. He asked us to pray for him, because he felt so sad about the many needy people who called or came to the church door.

We jumped to his aid. "You can't let these people get to you," said one of us. Another informed him, "In our church we have a policy that these calls all go to one of the elders. I don't ever get involved." I said, "I think I know those two. We gave them some money. I can't believe they're still making the rounds."

Then it hit me. "You're not asking us for our advice, are you?" I said in embarrassment. He shook his head. Humbled, we prayed for his heavy heart, as he had asked. In those moments, I realized that by loving those difficult people, people the rest of us preferred to ignore, our friend was sharing in the sufferings of Christ. Here we were trying to make his troubles go away, when Jesus wanted to meet him there. We hadn't been wise. We've all listened more carefully since then.

Wisdom Reframes the Picture

I saw a trade magazine once for framing stores. There were photographs of the winning entries from a contest the magazine had sponsored. Each framer got the same print but none of the entries looked remotely alike. It is astonishing how the size and color of a mat and frame change a picture. It even *feels* different. Pastoral wisdom is often a matter of reframing the picture people bring to us.

Scripture is always counterintuitive. Left to ourselves, we never would have thought of anything the Bible teaches. Who would have imagined, for example, that suffering—a "thorn in the flesh"—does not just build character but is actually where God stages His strength? Or what about Habakkuk, the prophet of God, who never dreamed that God would use the wicked to chasten his beloved people. When people come to us for help, or when our church is in turmoil, our job is to help them reframe the picture through the counterintuitive Word of God. "You see it this way," we say, "but look at this situation from God's perspective." We usually don't do God's people any favors when we just give them advice. Wisdom lies in helping them see their picture with God's frame around it.

GRACE, WITHOUT JESUS CHRIST, IS HOMELESS.

We're only able to reframe wisely if our own personal work in the Word does not go stale. The Bible has to be percolating already in my heart when someone comes to talk. We've all learned the uncanny way God briefs us in advance from Scripture for problems we never saw coming. Students in the counseling class I teach sometimes think they should make a catalog of Bible verses for every specific counseling situation so they'll be ready no matter what problem they hear. There are books that do that. But I find that if Scripture is fresh on my mind, no matter where I have been reading and studying, it comes to life in my counseling and leading. In many cases it isn't so much the biblical principle I need as the reframing of the picture only the Bible can accomplish.

Wisdom Is God's Gift to Pastors

Surely we have prayed like young Solomon for wisdom to lead God's people. I've noticed how often the wisdom of Scripture lies dormant within me until it blooms in a counseling session or conversation. The unique gift of wisdom is that we get to keep everything we learn. The more wisdom we dispense, the more wisdom we have. Plus, we are the repositories of the whole congregation's stories. We're the church's wisdom bankers.

It is the pastor's lot to hear and weigh life's most confounding problems. People want so badly to find someone wise. Not just glib advice givers, but someone deeply insightful, a shepherd who understands souls and can discern the heart's low frequencies and the overtones of God's grace.

GRACE. ESPECIALLY GRACE

Bill Moyers hosted a TV documentary on the hymn "Amazing Grace." For more than an hour I watched the story of John Newton's life and how he wrote this most famous hymn. Musicians of every stripe talked about its power. Alcoholics and convicts told how they leaned on it. But as far as I remember, in all that program the name of Jesus Christ was only mentioned once—when the epitaph on John Newton's gravestone was read.

Grace, without Jesus Christ, is homeless. To be clear, grace doesn't save a wretch like me. Jesus Christ does. It is the pastor's highest privilege to be an agent of the grace of our Lord Jesus Christ. God's grace in Christ is our calling, our work, our stock-in-trade.

Paul told Timothy to "do the work of an evangelist." We do that in our preaching and in our relationships. Pastors have the high privilege of leading people to trust Christ, and there is no work of grace more amazing than that. Some pastors *only* do the work of an evangelist, and perhaps that is their calling from God. But it is not the way a church is nourished. Years ago I sat for a year under a pastor whose every sermon was evangelistic. I don't know if anyone came to Christ through those sermons, but I don't think the church was very strong. Grace had become a monotone.

The greatest accomplishment of God's grace in Christ is to forgive and revive helpless and hopeless sinners. But grace does more than that. Pastors should dispense grace every chance we get. That is what this book is about. First, let's get oriented.

Grace Inbound

Before we can dispense grace, we must receive it. To begin with, of course, we must be born again. But after that, we pastors are often rather resistant to grace. The fact is, grace is really hard to take. By nature I'm like the elder brother in the story of the prodigal son, dutiful and disciplined. I *am* an elder brother. But unlike that self-righteous sibling in the story, I do not bridle when I hear of the Father's grace running to meet the wayward. I'm glad for that. I don't think God should be tougher on other sinners. My problem is that I think the Father should be much tougher on me. I've always been the straight arrow. I keep most of the rules. Once I asked my teenage son how he'd describe me to his friends. "Overachiever," he said. "Much given, much expected," is my assumption. That doesn't leave much room for grace.

It certainly isn't that I don't want God's grace. I do. But I just can't get past the fact that I don't deserve it. I want to be deserving. That's why I say grace is hard to take.

MEET PEOPLE WITH
YOUR POCKETS BULGING WITH GRACE.

Pastors should not sin so that grace might abound, of course; but we cannot shepherd the flock of God if we can't take grace ourselves. I sing benedictions in church sometimes (more about that later). One Sunday, after a whole service focused on the message of the cross, I sang the line, "Be strengthened by grace . . ." and my voice caught. Tears came. I suppose, if people noticed, they thought it was for their sakes, but I really wept for myself. After the week I'd had, I needed God's grace.

Grace is just as hard for the rest of God's people to take, so we need to keep at it. We're all like Peter, deeply uncomfortable with Christ washing our feet. That's why every sermon should be marinated in the grace of Christ. Sermons and counseling sessions that hammer have their place, but they're dangerous in heavy doses. God's people start taking on the prodigal's speech, "I am no longer worthy to be called your son; make me like one of your hired men" (Luke 15:19). We're not worthy, of course, but God never leaves us there. Pastors must not either.

44

Pockets Full of Grace

Jim was a gangly, grinning, retired blue-collar worker with the goofiest sense of humor I ever encountered. He had come to Christ in his sixties and, oh how he loved Jesus. His official ministry was usher, and he was born to do it. What especially endeared Jim to the church was that every Sunday, when the service was over, he would be waiting by the rear doors for the children. His jacket pockets bulged with Smarties, little rolls of candy, and every child got one. He loved the children so much that when he gave out that candy it could break your heart to watch. And we all watched.

Grace isn't candy, I know, but that is a wonderful picture for pastors. Grace isn't always about sin. Grace is God's favor lavished on those who couldn't get their hands on it by themselves. Meet people with your pockets bulging with grace.

Keep the grace of Scripture in your pockets. Don't be glib with it; don't turn God's words into platitudes. But as Proverbs 25:11 says, "A word aptly spoken is like apples of gold in settings of silver." Use Scripture to encourage and bless. Give out Bible words like small compasses to disoriented people, like water for runners, like God's smile for the sad.

Have a pocketful of the grace of sympathy and understanding. "That must have felt awful," you say. Or, "Thank you for being so faithful." "I would have been so scared. Were you?" "I've noticed in this trial how you have tried to trust the Lord."

We hand out grace, too, when we remember a visitor's name, the anniversary of a loved one's death, when we celebrate a good grade on an exam, or cheer for a wedding anniversary.

Always carry grace in your pockets. Be lavish with it, extravagant. There's plenty more where that came from.

When I was a young pastor, I heard someone say that a church takes on the personality of its pastor within three years. I don't know if that's true, but I do know that a pastor whose pockets are full of grace is likely to see his flock spread grace. God's grace is contagious. Being around grace is like being near someone who can't stop laughing. Pretty soon, you're laughing too.

"IN THIS TOWN
THERE IS A MAN OF GOD"

I was ordained on Sunday afternoon, December 27, 1981. My uncle, Dr. David Larsen, delivered the challenge. His text for me was 1 Samuel 9:6: "But the servant replied, 'Look, in this town there is a man of God; he is highly respected, and everything he says comes true. Let's go there now. Perhaps he will tell us what way to take.'" The mantle of that text was laid across my shoulders. Doing Wordwork for the Lord requires I have a good reputation and welcome people who long to know what way to take.

When we begin this daunting ministry, God gives us these three indispensable tools: authority, wisdom, and grace. But the greatest of these is grace. Grace, above all, is the pastor's foot in the door, the credential on our windshield that lets us park close to people's hearts.

Chapter Three

PUBLIC GRACE

A COUPLE who visited our church the first Sunday of January almost didn't come back. Half the church was out of town that holiday weekend. We had no worship team. Just one pianist and me to lead worship. It was old school, the way church services were when I was a kid. The couple who visited that day told me later that they weren't sure they wanted to go to a church where the pastor did everything. Can't say as I blame them, but I'm glad they stayed.

Gifted and godly people bring their worship arts to our churches, and we're all the richer for them. They give us new voices and new eyes. Pastors are better off, too, for not having to carry the full load of leading. However, there are parts of a worship service to which no one else brings quite the same touch as the shepherd of the flock.

Pastors whose only Sunday morning assignment is preaching are missing something, and so are their people. Shepherds who follow near to Jesus have an instinct about

His sheep that affects the way they do things. It isn't that pastors know God better than others who lead worship; but perhaps we know the people better. A good pastor carries a deep sense of people's burdens and failings and, I hope, the Good Shepherd's instinct for grace.

Years ago I read an article in the *Chicago Tribune* about a pep rally that the new head of the Chicago Sewers Department called for his workers. The headline said, "City tries to pump up its crews down under." You'd have thought the new boss was Joel Osteen. "Winning is not a sometimes thing," he shouted. "It's an all-the-time thing!" And the eight hundred people in the Plumbers Union Hall cheered enthusiastically.

IT DELIGHTS THE FATHER WHEN WE GIVE
PEOPLE A GOLD STAR NOW AND THEN.

Sometimes I look out over the congregation on Sunday morning and think about the dirty, difficult places God's people must work every week. Some offices, of course, are filthier than sewers. Some schools are darker than underground tunnels. Some families are toxic. A lot of Christians spend their week trying to keep the gunk off their hearts, trying to keep their souls from smelling like a cesspool. Good shepherds know. We think about where people have come from when they come to worship. If we are thoughtful, that will nuance how we grace what we do in the service. As my friend Brandon put it, "There is a degree of intimate knowing that a pastor brings."

Here are some worship assignments that pastors should be able to do with a unique touch.

Human Moments

Announcements feel like a bother. They can seem like billboards hiding the scenery of worship. But the announcement slot is a good time to remember that our congregation is a family. It delights the Father when we give people a gold star now and then, and the announcements are a good time to do that. "It's Joyce and Lowell's fiftieth wedding anniversary this week. Thank you for your example to us all!" And the church applauded. "School is starting. Would all our teachers, school staff, and home-schoolers stand? Let me take a minute and pray for you." "It is so good to see Jack here today. He's been out sick for a long time. Welcome home, Jack." "Today is Veteran's Day. Let's recognize all who are here who have served our country." Other worship leaders can honor these people, of course, but it is special to them when their pastor does it.

Heavies

One of my great pastoral regrets goes back to a September Sunday in 1994. Three days before, a USAir jet coming in for a landing at the Pittsburgh airport suddenly nosedived into a hillside, killing everyone on board—131 people. It happened twenty minutes from our church. USAir employed a lot of people in our congregation. One of our men was a gate agent nearby. One was a supervisor who had to meet with waiting families. One would work in the hangar where they brought the wreckage. Another worked for the FAA and would eventually investigate the whole event. The airline was on the financial ropes, and there was an immediate underlying fear that this disaster might put them out of business, costing thousands of jobs. The whole city mourned.

But my instincts that weekend were lousy. That Sunday morning I did not consider what had just happened to my flock. After all, I reasoned, no one in our congregation had lost anyone. I prayed about the loss but that was it. We should have taken plenty of time to grieve together in the Lord's presence, but I wanted to stick to the plan. I'm embarrassed to tell it.

PART OF WORSHIP IS RECOUNTING
GOD'S MIGHTY DEEDS, AND THE PASTOR
IS OFTEN THE CHURCH'S TELLER OF TALES.

In the fall of 2008 there was another crash. This time it was the markets. The younger people in our church were almost oblivious to the financial earthquake, living paycheck to paycheck as they do. But many in our congregation saw

years of careful saving drained. I knew people were frightened and I didn't want to make the same mistake twice. I felt
this was a time for me to comfort the church. I prayed for a
way to speak to them.

When the service started, I welcomed people and then
talked for a moment about the frightening things we were
seeing. Then I sang to them of God's care—no instruments,
just a little chorus, "He Careth for You." I read Scripture for a
few minutes, like I would in a hospital room, and prayed for
us to be able to rest in the Lord. Then I sang a verse and a
chorus of "His Eye Is on the Sparrow." Others could have done
all of those things at least as well as I, but no one else was
their pastor. We were all bolstered by God's sustaining grace.

Teller of Stories

The Psalms teach us that part of worship is recounting
God's mighty deeds. Those mighty deeds keep happening
among God's people, and the pastor is often the church's teller
of tales. Pastors circulate from life to life within the church,
picking up stories of God's work. Part of worship is telling
those stories to the glory of God. Sometimes before a song
or before I pray, I tell a story someone has told me. Other
times I do a brief interview, often right in the aisle. My associate pastor, Michael, recently asked Bob, a Gideon, to tell the
story of eager people receiving free New Testaments at the
county fair. During a recent sermon series from Proverbs 1–9,
I searched out people who especially loved reading the
Proverbs every day. Then I interviewed them on different
Sundays. One woman told of the lifelong impression her

mother made by reading a chapter of Proverbs every day to her kids. One of our businessmen talked passionately about how Proverbs shaped his life from his first days as a believer.

Like many churches, we put out a white rose and tell the story when someone is converted through a person in our congregation. One memorable Sunday recently we had two roses. I told the church of the fifty-year-old cleaning lady named Debbie whom one of our women led to Christ, and also introduced Andrew, a fifth grader, who had prayed with his parents a few days before. As I expected, the congregation clapped like they would for anyone who had just come home after a long time away.

These stories we tell don't take time from our worship; they *are* our worship. They tune up the songs we sing and illumine the Scripture we read.

The Table and the Bath

I am comfortable with others leading Communion or baptizing someone, but again these are privileges that pastors shouldn't miss. Often in our church, we serve Communion in trays passed down the rows. I love to stand there by the table and watch. There is time to look at particular people and remember how they came to Christ or what they've been through as believers. I'm humbled at the way they all turn their eyes toward me as I recite the familiar words, "The Lord Jesus, on the night he was betrayed, took bread . . ."

Sometimes we have people come forward to receive the elements. Usually there are four of us serving. Like so many other pastors have done, I look into the eyes of each person who stands expectantly before me. I can call most of them by name. "Janet, the blood of Christ shed for you." Sometimes my voice breaks.

Because we have a baptistery in the front of our church, we can baptize people during our morning service. We practice immersion and I meet the candidates as they each come down the steps into the water. I introduce them, and they share the story of their faith in Christ with the church. The pastoral moment is not when I baptize them. Others could do that. It is when I say a few words commending them to the church for a spiritual gift I've recognized or a particular way they touch others. I might mention how they've encouraged me or what promise I see in them as a believer. Then, after someone dear to them prays, I baptize them. Not long ago, on Easter Sunday, I baptized Drew. He is from a Christian home, but he had wandered far before the Father, seeing him a long way off, ran to meet him. After he was baptized and stood smiling beside me, I felt led by the Good Shepherd to say, "Some of you have been waiting a long time for a prodigal to come home. You see here what can happen. Take heart."

Hand Blessed

We hope our churches are blessing people often, but sometimes we do it with our hands. A new pastor is installed or ordained. A short-term missions team gathers on the platform. A new board of elders assembles to be recognized and commissioned. God dispatches one of our number to a new place of service, like when my longtime associate pastor, Jared, left to become a Navy chaplain. Christians have our own Bible expression for this that no one else uses: "the laying on of hands."

Some of these situations are weightier than others, but in each case representatives of the church are conveying God's grace to these people—grace for the journey and work, grace for the parting. The touch of our hands on heads and shoulders is the promise of God's call and blessing. Several people in our church may have hands for these commissionings, but a pastor should be among them, because the shepherd knows his sheep.

Our favorite blessing occasion is the dedication of children to the Lord. When parents bring their child to the platform, we are all reminded again what a precious and fragile gift a child is. The parents pray first, publicly committing their child to the Lord with a written prayer I give them. Then I pray, taking the baby in my arms or putting my hand upon the child's forehead and dedicating him or her to God. But our favorite part comes after that.

THIS BLESSING IS A UNIQUE
KIND OF STATEMENT, ITS OWN GENRE.
IT ISN'T A WISH. IT IS A DECLARATION.

Years ago I heard this idea from another church. While someone sings or plays—a lullaby perhaps—I carry the child down the aisles, row by row, from side to side, and the people, one by one, bless that precious little one. They reach far to touch his foot. "God bless you, David," they whisper. Hands gently touch her forehead. "God be with you, Lauryn." I see lips move, and their benedictions are so sweet I often have tears in my eyes. There is no other time quite like it in our church. The parents watch in wonder from the platform. They've warned me, many of them, that their baby might cry, and I promise that I'll bring him back to them if he does. But, amazingly, I do not remember that ever happening since I started doing this some twenty years ago. There's no particular reason I would need to be the one who carries this child through the congregation; when we have several children, others share the privilege. But I wouldn't miss it for the world and I think it is very important to the parents that their pastor does this.

"Let Us Stand for the Benediction"

Other than preaching, there is no privilege in a worship service I love more than pronouncing the benediction. I can't imagine ending a worship service with, "See you next week," or "You're dismissed," when I can offer our congregation God's blessing instead.

Through the mutual carelessness of pastors and their people, the words can cease being sacred gifts and become merely clergy code for the service's end, a congregational heads-up to collect their stuff. But, in fact, a benediction is so much more. This blessing is a unique kind of statement, its own genre. It isn't a wish. It is a declaration: "The Lord blesses you—He really does!" It doesn't tell us what God *will* do for us, but what God *is doing* ever and always for His people. It is God's vow.

Benedictions can be drawn directly from Scripture or shaped for that service. But believe me, when pastors stand before their people quietly, till everyone stops fidgeting, when we raise our hands over them (a gesture unique to church), and when we declare God's covenant care over them as emissaries of the Lord Himself, then God's people really are blessed. Grace settles on them afresh like dew.

WORSHIP LEADERS ARE LIKE SPOTLIGHT
OPERATORS, HELPING US ALL SHINE GLORY
ON GOD AT THE CENTER OF THE STAGE.

The benediction felt strange to me when I first pronounced it years ago. It was too weighty for my voice, too big for a man of my character. I felt peculiar—a little ostentatious—raising my hands over people like a priest. But that is what Aaron did from the very beginning, according to Leviticus 9:22: "Then Aaron lifted his hands toward the people and blessed them." So I do it, too, for the Lord's sake. I have memorized the biblical benedictions I use and I say them slowly, looking at faces. Some in the congregation hold their hands in front of them, cupped as though to receive a drink of water.

Perhaps some churches do not use the benediction because it sounds foreign to the unchurched they want to reach. But that is the point! It *is* foreign. Visitors won't hear God's blessing anywhere else. That is exactly why they should hear it when they are with us.

For what it's worth, I have taken to singing benedictions quite often. I know that isn't for everyone, but since I can sing passably, I've come to love mixing melody and blessing. I particularly like two written by Michael Card: "Barocha" (his rendition of Numbers 6:24–26) and a shortened version of "Grace Be with You All" (from Hebrews 13:20–21). All I can tell you is that sweet and holy things happen when I sing these blessings to God's beloved people. A young man who has only been in our church a couple of months told me, "When I first heard you sing the benediction as our shepherd I felt so loved."

Worship Is a Little *about Us*

Matt Redman has taught us to sing, "I'm coming back to the heart of worship, and it's all about You, all about You, Jesus." He's certainly right, but that doesn't mean worshipers should forget who they are. Worship wouldn't be better if we were all invisible. Worship is *sinners* celebrating salvation, *children* adoring their Father, the *blessed* effusive in their thanks to the Giver, the *weak* reminiscing of God's aid, and the *homesick* listening together for the trumpet and shout.

Worship is better when we keep in mind who we are.

What's more, true to His grace, God gives to us even when we want *Him* to receive all our attention. Does anyone ever come out of true worship thinking we put in more than we received? Worship leaders are like spotlight operators, helping us all shine glory on God at the center of the stage. But something else is going on. Remember what happened to the shepherds near Bethlehem? "And the glory of the Lord shone around them." We as the shepherds of God's people help our congregation see the glory of the Lord shining all around them. We grace God's worshipers with His delight in them and His timely Word in trouble, with the stories of His work among their brothers and sisters, with the bread and cup, and with water and holy hands.

Whether the worshipers in our churches come in from green pastures or up from the sewers, thanks to Christ they are privileged heirs of the King, priests of the Most High God, and the white-clad Bride of Christ. Shepherds help them remember that.

Chapter Four

PUBLIC GRACE
REFRESHED

WE TALK so often in church about Christ's forgiveness and love that it can start to feel like old news. Grace fades easily into the woodwork when it wears the same words every Sunday. God's grace becomes a wallflower.

That happens when pastors have an anemic gospel vocabulary. Years ago I participated in an ordination council where a young man was being quizzed on his doctrinal positions. He was asked, "What is justification?" He reached back for the old Sunday school play on words, "Justification is just-as-if-I'd never sinned." He sat back satisfied with his succinct, clever answer. As theological shorthand for *justified* it is okay, I guess; but if that's all the range a pastor can bring to the question, he needs to go back to his Bible.

Our worship can do that same disservice to God's grace, and for that matter, to all His wonders and works. I heard a worship leader say, "God's grace is just so . . . so . . . *amazing*!" I know he meant well, but I admit I thought, *That's the best you can do? Think about what you're going to say. Help us find words that aren't so threadbare—or don't say anything at all.*

NO PASTOR WITH A BIBLE

HAS ANY EXCUSE FOR GRAYSCALE GRACE.

Pastors, along with all who lead worship, are responsible before God to be sure the grace of our Lord Jesus Christ does not go monochromatic on Sunday mornings. Preeminently we point to Jesus' crucifixion, resurrection, and reign. We keep those familiar realities fresh by showing them from different angles. Yet Scripture bids us speak of the gospel as a many-splendored thing. Show the saints the blood-stained altar as well as the feast celebrating death's passing. Show them God's grace as a precious pearl and a just-found coin, wine from water and water from a rock. There is grace, too, in the dry bones stirring before Ezekiel, in Jacob's limp, and Mary's song. The gospel is in the twelve leftover bread baskets and in the King washing His servants' feet. No pastor with a Bible has any excuse for grayscale grace. It is, quite literally, a *dis*grace.

So what can a pastor do on Sunday mornings to refresh people's awareness of grace? It must not go without saying that preaching is our highest and best opportunity to set forth all the glories of God in Christ. We are Wordworkers assigned to "preach the Word." Beyond that, even if the pastor is not the main worship leader, these are ways we can help people see that God's mercies are new *this* morning.

Leave Room for Romance

In some churches, every element in worship is scheduled down to the minute. I don't think that is a bad thing so long as the planning comes after praying. But I do think grace likes a little elbow room in a service, some room to maneuver. I love the little prayer, "Lord, please do something this morning that isn't in the bulletin." That doesn't necessarily mean something that takes more time, but you can't rule it out either.

It's a little like romance. One of the secrets of romance is surprise, like showing up at your wife's office unexpectedly on the first day of spring with a bouquet of daffodils. Romance loves a surprise. So does grace. Pastors help Jesus and His bride romance one another with a little surprise in worship now and then. Go ahead—let's sing a song to our Beloved even if we don't have a slide ready with the words. Go ahead —spontaneously read some of the Lord's loving words to His church even if it wasn't planned. Go ahead—decide to hold everyone still and quiet for a moment so people "can know that I am God."

Let Grace Grin

The late humorist Erma Bombeck wrote in one of her most memorable columns:

In church the other Sunday I was intent on a small child who was turning around smiling at everyone. He wasn't gurgling, spitting, humming, kicking, tearing the hymnals, or rummaging through his mother's handbag. He was just smiling. Finally his mother jerked him around and in a stage whisper that could be heard in a little theatre Off-Broadway said, "Stop that grinning! You're in church!" With that, she gave him a belt and as the tears rolled down his cheeks added, "That's better," and returned to her prayers.[1]

Grace can behave like that child in church, and the pastor had better be ready to help everyone smile back. One Sunday years ago I was preaching and wanted to make a point about the way God draws people to himself. "Perhaps this very morning," I said, "somewhere in this valley someone who hasn't been in church in years woke up and said, 'Today, I'm going to find a church. I need to get back to God.'"

And at that moment—I kid you not—a visitor in the second row piped up, "Here I am!"

I was speechless for a moment. "Well, uh . . . there you have it!" I stammered. Grace turned around and grinned at everyone in church.

Visitors

We really want visitors to feel comfortable with us. We want them to know they are welcome and that we don't want to do anything to make them uncomfortable. We want them to come back. So we may get nervous when grace creates a bit of a scene. What if they see two people, hands on shoulders, praying earnestly in a corner? What if people start crying in the middle of a Jesus story? What if Communion seems too strange to them? What if we take an offering not because we need the money but because we're so grateful? What if we have the chutzpah to actually *bless* people in the Lord's name? Listen! Visitors do not ever need to be guarded from God's grace!

Then there are the people grace has invited to church, the broken and blind. You never know who God's grace will drag in. A friend of mine was so surprised to see an old high school friend of dubious reputation walk into church one Sunday that he blurted out, "What are *you* doing here?"

His friend might just as well have said, "Grace invited me."

Sometimes on Sunday mornings, lost sheep find us. Early one Sunday morning I stopped at the Mobil station near my house to get a cup of coffee. Sy, a shambling, sad guy was there, too, chatting with Muhammad, the attendant. "So what are you going to talk about today, Preacher?" Sy asked me.

I was preaching from Luke 15, so I told him, "I'm talking about how God searches for lost sheep."

Sy looked at me and replied plaintively, "I'm a lost sheep."

I invited him to church and a few weeks later he came—I found out this wasn't the first time.

When grace invites people to church, we pastors have an advantage. We're probably better positioned than anyone to help them connect with just the right believers. "Oh, let me introduce you to another military family," I might say. "You love running? So do Mike and Terry here." "India? You know we have some other people here from your part of India. Come and meet them." When Sy came, Ed and Elaine were just taking their seats. They are tenderhearted and patient with wounded people. I introduced them to Sy, and they welcomed him to sit with them then took him out for lunch after church. Pastors get to make introductions like that.

In the company of God's grace, pastors have to stay on their toes. God in His grace invites people to church, not only for their sake, but for ours.

The Ministry of Walking Around

When I was a young pastor, I was in a service where Dr. Warren Wiersbe was going to preach. It was a conference and I assume he didn't know most of the people there. Yet in the moments before the service started, he worked his way up and down the aisles and into the rows greeting people and shaking hands. I instinctively knew he was doing more than being friendly. He was pastoring, and he was doing a kind of sermon preparation for the people and for himself.

Now in the moments before our service, I do what I saw Dr. Wiersbe do. I try not to be loud because I don't want to disturb people who are praying before the service, but I take up "the ministry of walking around," as one colleague called it. I meet new people, find out how someone's child is doing in college, hug the grandmas, and tell the infrequent attenders how good it is to see them. I work hard at learning names because to use someone's name is a way we love them.

It is mostly small talk, I admit. But pastoral small talk isn't always so small. It only takes a moment to say, "I read about the layoffs at your company. Will they affect you?" Or, "Oh, this is your daughter? I've heard so many good things about you!" Sometimes pastoral care only takes a moment.

Pray Better

Praying publicly is an occupational hazard for pastors because it is so easy to pray on autopilot. We pray so often for the same things that it is hard to be thoughtful and focused. I've stood before the church and said, "Let us pray," bowed my head, and realized in that instant that I had no real idea of what we actually needed to say to God. I wonder if such prayers are not a nuisance to God. They call for His attention but then have nothing to say.

It isn't that we don't mean what we say, but that what we say doesn't mean much. We ought to be ashamed of ourselves the way we paste together clichés sometimes. What do we think God will do with those petitions? What's more, what are we teaching God's people about how they should pray? We do not have to find stately and lyrical language (though it wouldn't hurt), but we need to speak to God thoughtfully and reverently.

One evening in a board meeting, our elders were praying for people in the congregation. Bob began to pray slowly, deliberately, "Almighty Father, who in Your great mercy gladdened the disciples with the sight of the risen Lord . . ." We weren't used to hearing language like that. He paused and went on, "Give L— such knowledge of His presence with her, that she may be strengthened and sustained by His risen life and serve You continually in righteousness and truth . . ." Another brief pause, "through Jesus Christ Your Son, our Lord."

After his amen, the room fell silent. Later, as we were leaving, one of the brothers said, "Bob, I so appreciated your prayer." He replied, "Thank you, but those weren't my words.

That was from *The Book of Common Prayer.*" Bob's spare, weighty prayer had a kind of gravitational pull on all of us. It drew our prayers into its center, not because it was a prayer from a book but because it was a prayer from Bob's heart.

SPEAK GRACE IN THE TENDERHEARTED
TONES OF THE ONE WHO WAS ANOINTED
TO COMFORT ALL WHO MOURN
AND PROVIDE FOR THOSE WHO GRIEVE.

Shepherds can find no better prayers than those in the Psalms, straight from the hearts of other good shepherds of God's people. Here are prayers that not only equip us all with God-given words but also reshape our souls as we pray. They tell us what we may pray and what we should pray. They are prayers that give us every reason for faith. Surely God says "amen" when we pray them.

I love this passage from the beginning of Frederick Buechner's novel, *On the Road with the Archangel*:

> I am Raphael, one of the seven archangels who pass in and out of the presence of the Holy One, blessed be he. I bring him the prayers of all who pray and those who don't even know that they're praying.
>
> Some prayers I hold out as far from me as my arm will

reach, the way a woman holds a dead mouse by the tail when she removes it from the kitchen. Some, like flowers, are almost too beautiful to touch, and others so aflame that I'd be afraid of their setting me on fire if I weren't already more like fire than I am like anything else. There are prayers of such power that you might almost say they carry me rather than the other way round—the way a bird with outstretched wings is carried higher and higher on the back of the wind. There are prayers so apologetic and shamefaced and half-hearted that they all but melt away in my grasp like sad little flakes of snow. Some prayers are very boring.[2]

Thank God that He hears and interprets all our prayers, however brief or mangled our words might be, or even when there are no words at all. But when we are publicly helping our flock pray, we should try to choose our words more carefully. We need to think about what we ask of God.

Whatever language we use, we would be wise to think before we ask people to bow their heads. The Bible tells us to "pray in the Spirit." I take that to mean that we should expect the Breath of God to animate our prayers and the mind of Christ to give them substance and faith. Such prayers have a sacred elegance and a gracious eloquence that move the hand of God and form the hearts of His people.

Be Kind

Sometimes it seems like the pastoral default, especially in preaching, is to chew people out. Or at least to be constantly challenging them. Unfortunately, our sense of holy responsibility can give our words a cutting edge. But God told Isaiah, "Comfort, comfort my people, says your God. Speak tenderly to Jerusalem, and proclaim to her that her hard service has been completed, that her sin has been paid for" (Isaiah 40:1–2). I know there are times when the stern word of God must drop like a hammer, but surely in the church of Jesus Christ it shouldn't be too often.

No one in the whole congregation is better positioned to comfort God's people than their shepherd. We likely know more of their dark nights and predatory fears than anyone else. We've seen how sin has crushed them and how helpless or confused they often feel. So speak kindly to them. Don't just be nice. Speak grace in the tenderhearted tones of the One who was anointed to comfort all who mourn and provide for those who grieve.

There is no doubt that Jesus' disciples can be faithless and hardhearted, but I think most of God's people really want to love Jesus well. They really want to trust God when things go badly. They want to worship more wholeheartedly and to pray more effectively. Thanks to the hardworking grace of God, most Christians in the church I serve are not like the proud Pharisee, praying so that everyone but God hears. If anything, they tend to stand afar off, a little unsure of His invitation to come boldly to God's throne of grace.

So speak kindly to them. Don't just be chipper and upbeat. Don't just get them to smile. What if we took our cues from Paul? "Good morning, you whom Jesus loves so much! This week I have thanked God for you because you are so rich in His grace! I thanked Him for all the gifts you have been given through Christ. Isn't it wonderful to be loved by our heavenly Father!"

What if we graced God's people next Sunday by saying, "I know that some of you have been on the receiving end of life's heavy hand this week, but do you know how God sees you? You are His chosen people. You are His royal priesthood. You are His holy nation, God's special possession. And do you know what that means for us in these next moments? It means that we get to declare the praises of Him who called you out of darkness into His wonderful light. Brothers and sisters, once you were not a people, but now you are the people of God; once you had not received mercy, but now you *have* received mercy. What a privilege it is to be here together with you!" (from 1 Peter 2:9–10).

NO ONE COMES TO CHURCH
WHO DOESN'T NEED TO DRINK DEEPLY OF GRACE.

Be kind whether you make announcements, pray, or preach. Be gentle and understanding. Remember that Jesus invites the weary and burdened to find rest in Him. Go easy on the guilt unless God's Spirit and God's Word require it. Then be sure to speak the truth *in love* and be sure to lead them to grace. Lighten up on the "oughts" once in a while.

Some of the best pastoral advice I ever heard, outside of Scripture, is, "Be kind, for every person you meet is fighting a great battle." No one knows who said that first, but blessed is the congregation whose pastor believes it. Kindness in a worship service, or anywhere else for that matter, seems to help people let their guard down so grace can do its work.

"That's Why I Need It."

It is easy to forget how deeply people need God's grace when they come to church. The grace of God in Christ does far more than convert us. And while there is no substitute for preaching, grace can do more than preach.

Years ago a couple started slipping unnoticed into our worship services. They were also seeing me for counseling because of a great grief they had suffered. They had another church home, but it had become a toxic place and they were taking a kind of sabbatical. They had been hurt by harsh accusations and they were bleeding from their grief. One week when they came to see me the wife said, "I didn't like what you said before Communion last Sunday."

What she meant was part of the warning I typically gave. "If there are people whom you haven't forgiven," I had said, "you should not take Communion because it is a celebration of forgiveness."

She looked at me with tears in her eyes and said, "That's why I *need* it. That's why I *need* to take Communion, because they are so hard to forgive."

You can make of that what you will. For my part, I have reexamined Scripture and think now that the Scripture does not warn sinful people not to take Communion, but rather puts on notice those who desecrate the holy meal by their crass and unloving behavior. But in any case, I have never forgotten that heartache. No one comes to church who doesn't need to drink deeply of grace. As their shepherds we need to be sure that we do all we can to keep God's grace fresh.

Chapter Five

PORTABLE GRACE

MAY 31, 1985, was a Friday. We had an early evening dinner meeting at church where people could meet an associate pastor candidate. The weather had been stormy. After a ferocious downpour an eerie calm settled in. The phone in the kitchen rang, and Ronnie, who answered, was told a tornado had just mowed through his neighborhood. Everyone scattered for their homes alarmed. We went with some friends and had no sooner gotten to their house than there was a knock on the door.

Our friend Roy was a surgeon, and at the door was another surgeon from our church, Bob. The tornadoes had done serious damage. People were hurt and the hospital's emergency plan had been activated. Roy and Bob left immediately for the nearby hospital. I immediately thought, *I wonder if a pastor should go, too.* Some *pastor. Any pastor other than me.* Now, as I tell it, I'm not sure why, but that night I really did not want to go. I was frightened, I think, of what I might face. I dawdled awhile, and finally gave in.

Since it was a Friday evening when the tornadoes struck, many people—kids especially—were out for the evening. And in that time before cell phones, their families couldn't reach them. Not knowing what else to do, many people went to the hospital, just in case. When I walked into the lobby there were groups clustered everywhere. They were anxious. They scavenged for any information they could find. Occasionally, one of the hospital staff would come out and shout something like, "Is there anyone from the Martin family here? The Martin family?" People looked around sympathetically.

I didn't know what else to do so I swallowed hard, whispered a prayer for help, and walked up to the first group. "I'm a pastor," I said. "Is there anything I can do for you?" I remember wondering if they would ask suspiciously what church I was from or be offended by my forwardness. But no one was. "Would you like me to pray for you?" I asked.

"Yes, please," they said. Every group I approached said that. I prayed for their loved ones by name and asked for God's peace and help. No one asked what church I was from. Everyone wanted prayer, and everyone thanked me. I wondered why I had been so reluctant.

"You Don't Ask!"

I've been saying that when God calls pastors He endows us with a certain spiritual instinct for the work, a shepherd's heart. That said, I'm not suggesting that all pastoral responsibilities come naturally to us. I have trouble taking grace on the road. I like organizing and studying quietly at my desk. I love everything about Sunday mornings. While I like being with people at the hospital or in their homes, I just don't always have the gumption to get out the door. Lots of pastors are just the opposite. It's like grace is burning a hole in their pockets and they can't wait to go out and find someone to spend it on. But I've had a lot to learn.

I got a call at church one summer evening when I was a young assistant pastor. Our senior pastor was away so I was in charge. Art was calling to say that his college-aged son, Tom, who was working on a garbage truck for a summer job, had been seriously injured when his truck was hit by a train. He was in a coma at the hospital.

"Do you want me to come?" I asked.

There was about a half a beat before he said, "No, you don't need to do that. Just ask the church to pray."

Half an hour later, people started arriving for a meeting and I spread the word. Jim, a wise and direct lay leader, asked me, "Are you going to the hospital?"

"Art said not to," I replied.

He looked at me, incredulous. "You don't ask!" he exclaimed. "You're the pastor. You go!"

GRACE IS SOCIAL. JESUS LOVES
BEING WITH PEOPLE. SO PASTORS LEARN TO GO.

My public style is very warm, so most folks don't realize I am really weak at sympathy. Sadly, sometimes people in our church learn the hard way when I fail them. I've been a pastor for nearly thirty-five years and I'm more responsive than I used to be. But I often have to resort to a quiet little test question: "What would a sympathetic pastor do?" The sympathy to go to the hurting is the first step grace takes. It is pretty hard to help when I keep my distance.

God expects pastors to get gospel grace out the church door. Grace is portable. Grace is social. Jesus loves being with people. So pastors learn to go.

Spiritual Medics

Pastors are spiritual medics. We take the phone call, then we grab our jackets and Bibles and head into the crisis. On the way our hearts ache and pound at the same time. What will this be like? What will we say? We know that people call us because they hope we will bring the Lord to them in a dark hour. It's a lot to ask.

I hadn't been a pastor long when one of the young adults in my group called me. "I'm in the hospital," she said, her voice very subdued. "The psych ward. I admitted myself. I've been suicidal." I knew I had to go visit, but I had never been to a psych ward and I didn't know what to expect. After I passed through the locked doors, I found myself in what seemed like a sad dorm. My friend told me why she was there. It was the first time I'd heard what abuse could do to a heart.

Easter was the following Sunday and she wouldn't be released in time to come to church. I asked if she'd like me to bring Communion, and she said she would like that very much. Then she asked, "Would you mind if I invited some others? There are other Christians here."

So I returned on Good Friday afternoon with my new small portable Communion set. Six little cups, a small gold container for bread, and a tiny bottle of grape juice. There were six of us, bruised souls all, but them especially. Communion doesn't change much from one time to the next, but I've never been with a circle of people like that since. Those dear saints were very nearly hopeless. Yet they gathered because they believed that Jesus loved them and died for them. Their dark places were not too dark for Him. I brought them the tangible taste of the gospel's promise. However, as you can imagine, I felt I got the best of grace that afternoon.

WHEN CHRISTIANS SPEAK TO EACH OTHER IN
PSALMS, HYMNS, AND SPIRITUAL SONGS OUR
HEARTS HARMONIZE WITH THE LORD.

We pastors are thrust into confounding situations. Some are terrible, brutal, heartbreaking. Some are just weird. I don't have to tell fellow pastors how many times I had no idea what to do or say next. Long ago, I laid claim to what Jesus said in Mark 13:11, "Whenever you are arrested and brought to trial, do not worry beforehand about what to say. Just say whatever is given you at the time, for it is not you speaking, but the Holy Spirit." Many times I have prayed, "Lord, I am not facing a judge, but I am in this scary situation in Your name, and I don't know what to say. Please give me the words for this hour by Your Holy Spirit." And He does.

Ginny was unresponsive when I visited her in a respiratory intensive care ward. She had multiple sclerosis and I didn't know what to do. I doubted that she could even understand if I read Scripture.

I had first gotten to know Ginny singing in the choir. There was a spot in the front row for her wheelchair. So that day by her bedside I thought, *I should sing for her.* But then I looked around. There were four beds in that ward. There were curtains, but most of them were pulled back to make one big busy room. Nurses and technicians rushed in and out. *There's no way I can sing with all these people around,* I thought. But Jesus insisted, so I took a deep breath and started. I think I sang, "Jesus Loves Me" and "It Is Well with My Soul." I pitched one hymn too high and had to stop. I forgot the words in the middle of another. I'm used to singing in public, but this was a different story. I sang for Ginny for quite a while. My self-consciousness went away and I realized I was doing all those other folks a favor—a grace—because they listened too.

I sang for another lady like Ginny once and when I left, the nurse attending her said her blood pressure had stabilized while I was there. I didn't even have David's harp!

For several weeks I visited Bob in the intensive care unit.

We would talk. I'd read Scripture and pray. And eventually I think I sang every song I could remember—and some I couldn't. One time as I was wrapping up I said, "Bob, I'm sorry, but I have to get going."

"That's okay," he replied, "When you're not here, I can still hear you singing."

I hope you understand that people do not respond like that because my voice is so good. It is because when Christians speak to each other in psalms, hymns, and spiritual songs our hearts harmonize with the Lord. Some prayers are best sung. Try it and see for yourself. If you really cannot sing, bring someone with you who can.

Welcome at Work

There are a lot of doors that open to shepherds. The first church I served had a lot of businessmen. At first those suited, sophisticated guys intimidated me, but as friendships developed I got up my nerve and decided to take a one-day pastoral road trip. I arranged to ride the train into Chicago with one man. I met another for mid-morning coffee, another for lunch, a fourth around 3:00 p.m. Then I rode home on the train with one more.

I was afraid I'd be bothering these busy executives. I wondered if it would be embarrassing to them if their pastor showed up in their offices. But it was just the opposite. They were honored that I came. They introduced me to their coworkers. They wanted to tell me about their work, show me their offices, and let me see the pictures and plaques on their walls. When I asked if I could pray for them in their offices, I realized that likely no one had ever done that for them before. Since then I've visited lots of people at their jobs, and it is always the same.

When we take grace on the road, wherever it is we go, we need to remember some things.

First, don't be embarrassed by Jesus. In secular places I feel a subtle temptation to water down the gospel's wine, to be a little *too* discreet. After all, this isn't church. But we help people normalize Christ's presence in their workplace. When we speak of Him naturally and personally over a desk or a lunchroom table, maybe they will too.

Do Wordwork. Ask God to help you naturally weave biblical truth into your visit. Choose a short passage of Scripture you can read if there is an opportune moment. Ask your friend what they have learned about the Lord and the gospel in this place. Ask them what is hardest about being a Christian on the job. Encourage them in the Lord.

Pray for people whenever you can. Think about what you've seen and heard with them. You might be able to pray to the surface the frustrations, sorrows, and sins that lie beneath their veneer. Draw up promises and blessings from Scripture like water from a spring. Invite Jesus into what are often godless places.

Honor their work. When you see skill, say so. "That machine is really complicated! How long did it take you to learn this?" When you sense how draining their job must be, acknowledge that. After I toured a steel mill, I had a new appreciation for the toll it took on our men who worked there. Tell God's saints you can see how valuable they are in this place, not only to their company but also to Christ. "It is obvious how people respect you here. You've worked a long time to build up a reputation like that."

Salt

I've never been great at evangelism. I don't mind sharing my faith, but I think there are so many people in my life that I am subconsciously reluctant to go out looking for more. Nonetheless, I realized I had to do something. Other pastors coach Little League or join Rotary. Hanging out at a doughnut shop was more my speed. I started going early in the mornings to read and drink coffee. And guess what? I made friends who weren't Christians. Other Christians do that all the time, but I had not. I did learn that being a pastor among unbelievers gave me some advantages my fellow believers probably don't have.

WHEN IT COMES TO SALTY LANGUAGE,
I THINK GOD HAS GIVEN US THE ADVANTAGE.

One morning the owner introduced me to a brash guy I'd seen many times. "Lee, this is Lou. Lou, this is Lee. He's a pastor."

Lou smiled devilishly. "You're a pastor, huh?" he said. "So

I suppose you don't like words like . . . ," and he unleashed a string of vulgarities meant to shock me.

"Well," I said, "I like those words about as much as you like words like sin, hell, repentance, and righteousness."

He grinned at me, speechless for a second, before he said, "Good one." And just like that, we became friends. I'm pretty sure he had never had a pastor friend before. When it comes to salty language, I think God has given us the advantage.

Now I hang out at a local Einstein's Bagels. I've been going for well over ten years, often several times a week. The manager cuts me a break on coffee. I don't evangelize much in the usual sense of the word, but I do try to be salty. People there know me and know what I do. Many of us are friends.

I NEED TO KNOW PEOPLE WHO DON'T GO
TO CHURCH VERY OFTEN. THEY'RE GOOD FOR ME.

I met a guy there years ago I always called Two-Phone Joe. The first time I saw him I was sitting at an outdoor table. When he came out he had a cell phone pressed between his shoulder and ear, talking a blue streak. He had a cup of coffee in one hand, a Coke in the other, and *another* phone on his belt. When he put his cup down to hang up, I grinned at him and said, "Man, you've got to relax a little!" And that's how my friendship got started with one of the most hyper guys I've ever known.

Joe and I talked often. Actually, Joe ranted and raved and I mostly listened. Once I was reading when he came in, assaulting his phone as usual. He talked, loud and angry, the whole time he was in line and then, after he sat down, he kept arguing for the whole coffee shop to hear. It was about his impending divorce. When he finally got off the phone, I said, "Joe, come here."

"What?" he barked guardedly.

"Sit down here," I repeated.

"Why?" he asked, but he sat down.

"Joe, I don't know if anyone has ever done this for you before, but I am going to pray for you right now." Joe's eyes got big and he looked at me like I was crazy. Before he could run, I just put my hand on his arm and quietly prayed for a few seconds, asking God to quiet Joe and to give him peace.

"Thank you," Joe said softly, and I wondered if that might have been the first holy moment in Joe's entire tumultuous life. I think I got away with it because I was a pastor.

I started hanging out in a coffee shop, in part, because I need to know people who don't go to church very often. They're good for me. I watch the world go by from my corner table. Even when I have no conversations I catch a flavor of the lives all around me. I watch droop-shouldered salesmen, aggressive young executives, moms with their kids, teenagers mesmerized by their cell phones. I realize how hard it is to be an immigrant, and I watch parents trying to connect with their kids over a muffin. I have become much more sympathetic—

and more patient. I love non-Christians better than I used to.

Matthew 9:36 tells us: "When [Jesus] saw the crowds, he had compassion on them, because they were harassed and helpless, like sheep without a shepherd." I know some of those harassed and helpless people. We have coffee together. Often, I am the only shepherd they know.

Sometimes people open up to me more than they would to others because they know I'm a pastor. They let me ask personal questions. They are glad when I say I'll pray for them. Sometimes they ask me Bible questions or what I'm preaching on.

I must also say that some of these friends have cared for me when my own burdens were heavy. In all this, I'm learning another facet of grace. I am salt, but I am also being salted.

There was a guy who came in almost every morning. Mike would get his coffee and work the crossword puzzle. Once when he was stumped on the last few words the assistant manager pointed him to me. She had often seen me reading so she said, "Ask that guy. He's smart."

He strolled over and without a word, he flopped the folded newspaper on my table. Also without a word, I filled in the puzzle's missing words and handed it back. That's how our friendship started, doing puzzles. He said he was like the starting pitcher and I was the closer. From time to time we talked about more serious matters. One day we had done the puzzle and he was walking out. I was just kidding him about his puzzle routine when I called after him, "Man, you've got to get a life!"

He stopped, the door half open, and just looked at me for

a minute. Then he said, "You're right. I need to get a life." In the weeks after that he told me he had started going to church. When he took a new job and it was clear we wouldn't see each other anymore, he invited me down to see the new place that had hired him.

These folks aren't targets for me. I really enjoy knowing them. Their lives are interesting. I enjoy our visits, and we laugh a lot. I like to think I'm messing with their stereotype of an evangelical pastor.

There are people in our church and yours, I suspect, who are much bolder and more effective in evangelism than I am, but being a pastor gives me a shepherd's sense about people. And having unchurched friends makes me a better pastor.

I don't go to Einstein's all those mornings just because I like the coffee. I go because I need to taste the life of people around me and perhaps give them a taste of Jesus. When I sit there, I often think of part of a poem by Beatrice Cleland that I came across long ago:

> For me, 'twas not the truth you taught,
> To you so clear, to me so dim,
> But when you came to me you brought
> A sense of him.
> And from your eyes he beckons me,
> And from your lips his love is shed,
> Till I lose sight of you, and see
> The Christ instead.

Chapter Six

DECORATING
WITH GRACE

I OCCASIONALLY WATCH a reality television show
called *Property Brothers* about twin brothers, Jonathan and
Drew, who help people find, buy, and renovate homes. They
specialize in extreme fixer-uppers. As the brothers show the
prospective buyers various homes, the people looking to buy
almost always have trouble believing that they could ever feel
at home in the ugly and damaged house they are seeing.

My favorite part in each episode is when Jonathan uses
computer modeling to show them how radically the space
could be transformed into a beautiful home they could love.
He shows them what they couldn't imagine themselves. There
on the computer screen the old room is stripped down to the
floorboards and a new room is built layer by layer, even with
the accent pieces, right before their eyes. "I can't believe it!"
the wife says. "That's amazing!" marvels the husband. "You
could really do that? On our budget?"

Grace does that for the church. The people, I mean, not

the drywall and joists. Grace is the church's interior decorator, the ultimate renovation expert. "Once you were not a people," Peter recalled, "but now you are the people of God." Paul points to the rubble of old dividing walls and says, "You are being built together to become a dwelling in which God lives by his Spirit." Deep beneath the church is the foundation stone, Jesus Christ, and tight up against His great cornerstone lay the granite teachings of the apostles and prophets. All of it is a gift to the saints, undeserved and unsought.

Bezalel's Kin

God employs grace-skilled Wordworkers to help build His temple. Pastors use our unique spiritual trade, Wordworking, to make sure the people of God whom we serve are built to the specifications of His holiness and mercy in Christ. We are blessed to be part of the answer to Paul's great prayer in Ephesians 3, that the church, "being rooted and established in love, may have power, together with all the saints, to grasp how wide and long and high and deep is the love of Christ, and to know this love that surpasses knowledge—that you may be filled to the measure of all the fullness of God."

Architects are sometimes identified by the design approach they follow, like the Prairie School inspired by Frank Lloyd Wright. The spiritual architecture of God's church gets its inspiration, you might say, from the Tabernacle School. The church is Christ's Body, God's temple, and His holy priesthood. So it stands to reason that as a people we would bear the design of the Tabernacle.

Think about the Tabernacle's courtyard and holy rooms, the precious metals, jewels, fabrics and designs. Think about the furniture, each piece symbolizing an essential aspect of the relationship of God and His people. Think about the priests, their garments and responsibilities, and about the sacrifices and celebrations. Every detail mattered. In both explicit and implicit ways, the Tabernacle declared the holiness and grace of God. It stirred memories of the world God had created, preached God's remedy for sinful hearts and creation, and promised the hope of glory. It was an architectural prophecy of Christ. Now, God's people, alive with Christ, display that same detailed interior design.

Remember Bezalel, the craftsman charged with building the Tabernacle? God said in Exodus 31:3–5, "I have filled him with the Spirit of God, with skill, ability and knowledge in all kinds of crafts—to make artistic designs for work in gold, silver and bronze, to cut and set stones, to work in wood, and to engage in all kinds of craftsmanship." Bezalel and his right-hand man, Oholiab, were our pastoral second cousins, a long way removed. We do the kind of work they did, only with the precious people of God. We help craft God's people into a "dwelling in which God lives by his Spirit."

Our job is to show believers that while God's grace starts with the Altar of Sacrifice and ends at the Mercy Seat of the Almighty, there is much more to the holiness and grace of God. We traffic through all of Scripture to show them that Christians are a royal priesthood called to serve God with hands washed clean, in the lamplight of truth, lifting the incense of prayer, and breaking bread with the Lord. We teach them the wonder of coming boldly to God through the curtain Christ tore when He died. We work with the Holy Spirit to build these and other sacred privileges into our fellowship together so that we are a temple befitting the presence of God.

When a church mirrors the heavenly temple of God with the Holy Spirit moving freely among us, our congregation becomes a kind of collective preacher. When outsiders come into a congregation that is inwardly designed and equipped to be God's temple, they know something is different. They sense the Spirit of God among the people of God. Like Paul said of himself in Romans 15:16, the church is called "to be a minister of Christ Jesus to the Gentiles with the priestly duty of proclaiming the gospel of God, so that the Gentiles might become an offering acceptable to God, sanctified by the Holy Spirit."

GOD IS LIKE THE ART INSTRUCTOR. PASTORS AND CHURCH LEADERS ARE EACH AT OUR EASELS IN A STUDIO AROUND JESUS, WHO IS OUR MODEL.

Recently a young man named Alec showed up at church because his Christian friend John invited him. Alec, by his own admission, was somewhere between an agnostic and an atheist. He came that first morning in his black Slayer T-shirt with his guard up. But even before church started, God's people got to know him. Nancy, a grandma, surprised him with a hug. He listened to us sing and pray. He saw how we enjoyed Christ and one another. After church Guy told Alec how he had come to Christ.

When it was time to go, Alec told his Christian friend John, "I thought all Christians were arrogant blankety-blanks, but I've never met people like these before." Then he asked John, "Do you come here every week?" and when John said he did, Alec asked, "Can I come with you again?"

We gave him a Bible and God just moved into Alec's life. The Lord convicted him of sin and brought the Scriptures to life for him. Only a couple of weeks later John and Alec waited for me after the service. Alec asked if he could talk to me sometime because he "wanted to convert." Fifteen minutes later the three of us met in my office and went over the gospel carefully. Then Alec prayed and "converted." Jesus saved Alec, of course; but Alec first saw Jesus in his friend John, and then in the whole church. My sermons didn't have much to do with Alec's conversion. But my pastoral work, like Bezalel's, helped build a priestly, preaching church that displays the glorious architecture of grace.

Paint

I came to the church I now serve from a congregation four times bigger. At first I felt the change most sharply in worship. There were just two of us to take turns leading worship, and we had two pianists. No guitar or drums. No choir or organ. No screens or projector. We had a hymnal and a praise chorus book in the pew racks. I know lots of churches do with less, but I had gotten used to the resources of a larger congregation.

I remember saying to the Lord, "How do You expect us to worship when this is all we have?!"

And if I heard Him correctly God said, "Ex*cuse* Me? Just what is it you *need* to worship Me?"

I think what I actually meant was, "How do You expect us to compete with other churches who 'do' worship better than we can?" It sounds terrible put like that, but I think that was it.

Around that time, I was thinking one day of a painter, a palette in one hand and a brush in the other. I imagined planning a worship service—or leading a church, for that matter—like painting a picture. God is like the art instructor. Pastors and church leaders are each at our easels in a studio around Jesus, who is our model. "Paint a church that looks like Jesus," God says. Then He starts squeezing paint out of tubes onto each of our palettes.

I'm already imagining what my church painting will look like when I see the pigments God gave me. This can't be right!

"Wait," I said, "I need more colors than that. There's no red. I can't paint a church without red. I'll have to go borrow red from someone else." I notice that other pastor-painters are having the same problem. They are also missing colors they figure they will need. Most of us are thinking God has been a little too sparing if He expects masterpieces.

Then God, our art instructor, says, "I've given you all you

need to portray Christ through your church. Just paint with the colors I gave you."

That line has become a motto for our church: We will paint with the colors God gives us. It is a way of thinking that pervades our whole church. We think about that when we're trying to discern new ministry direction or how longtime ministries can be more effective. Generally, our leaders don't decide what kinds of ministries we should have or what they should look like. We keep looking at the people God gives us, with their backgrounds, passions, and spiritual gifts, and imagine what our church could paint with those colors.

This philosophy of ministry is easiest to see in our worship services. Instead of trying to be contemporary, blended, or traditional in worship, we try to be *us*, full of grace. Many churches choose their worship style and music in order to appeal to the kinds of people they want to draw. Many use only their best musicians. I get that. But we have decided not to do it that way. We decided that, whenever we can, we will use the people God gives us, as many of them as possible, regardless of whether they play a bass or a bassoon. I know this approach isn't for everyone, but you might be surprised at how wide the appeal is, *especially* to unchurched people who come. Contrary to our assumptions, outsiders don't actually come to church for the music. Whether they know it or not, God brought them to see Jesus.

For example, Nathaniel brings his operatic training to his solos while Daniel sings winsome, sweet songs he has written. John reads Scripture as though he carried a treasure with his voice. Occasionally, a gospel quartet gets us all smiling for the joy of heaven. Kay puts things on our Communion table that make us think. I would guess that forty people or more are involved in our services over the course of a month. Every service isn't a masterpiece, but I think God is pleased with the unique painting we give Him.

One of my favorite parts of being a pastor is painting with people. I don't usually have a strong sense of vision (one of my least favorite words), but I often see the makings of a ministry before others do because I have the best vantage point. Pastors often see the strings God is pulling before others do. We get to make introductions and connections that God has prepared.

One day I was telling a young woman about some of our ministries when somehow it came out that what she really loved was working with senior adults. Only a day or two before someone else had told me the same thing, and a week later I heard it from a third person. I started thinking about how many people in our church have experience working with older people. Plus, we have several who live in a nearby retirement community and care a great deal about their neighbors. I've been preaching there for a couple of years and have made some great friends. My associate pastor, Michael, and I realized we might be on to something.

We called half a dozen nursing and rehab centers right around us, and three of them *begged* us to come and lead services or to just visit with people. An activities director told us, "We have someone who comes and reads from *Chicken Soup for the Soul*, but we need someone to come in here and do a Jesus talk." So that's what we do.

We didn't dream up this ministry. We had no particular vision for it at first. In fact, it really wasn't on our radar. But we do what so many pastors do: We looked at the colors God gave us and helped our church paint.

Saying Yes

What pastor hasn't had someone come up and say, "I have this great idea for a new ministry"? I admit I cringe a little when I hear things like that. It isn't because I'm averse to new ideas. It's because I'm averse to more work!

There are a variety of good reasons why we don't give equal weight to every idea. But sometimes God is behind one of those crazy ideas. I've watched the property brothers on TV plead with prospective home buyers to see past the mess in a room to imagine how warm and inviting it could be with some work. Some just don't buy it. Pastors can be like that. God brings someone along with a great opportunity, solution, or vision; but sometimes we shut them down because we just can't see it.

"LET'S BE A CHURCH THAT SAYS YES."

About a month before we moved from our church in western Pennsylvania, Bobby talked to me about an idea he had for an outreach event. Bobby loved sharing Christ and he was into cars big time. In fact, he was a professional drag racer. He wanted the church to host a car cruise where enthusiasts show off their customized cars. (I was yawning already.) He thought he could get a big-name Christian driver to share the gospel. He said he could bring his funny car and do a burn-out down the road that ran by the church. The church people could serve beverages and hot dogs. He thought he could pull something together by summer. Then he asked what I thought.

Well, I thought it was a crazy idea. But I was moving soon, and this fell into the "what could it hurt to try?" category, so I just said, "Sounds interesting. Go for it." I didn't realize God in His grace had whispered the idea to Bobby. A few months later, I heard that more than a thousand people showed up to look at cars, watch a burn-out, and eat hot dogs on a summer afternoon. A well-known Christian driver shared Christ and people believed the good news. The publisher of *Christian Motorsports Illustrated* showed up and wrote a cover article on the event so other churches could model it. That crazy cruise idea became a significant annual outreach. It wasn't just that people came. People came to Christ.

Once years ago, when our staff was puzzling over some new idea, my associate pastor at the time, Paul, said simply, "Let's be a church that says yes." That was grace talking! And that has become another of our core values.

A couple of years after that, I called an OTSP (on the same page) meeting to help all our various leaders work through our philosophy of ministry. One of the things we went over was being a church that says yes. They had all heard it before, and they all nodded agreeably.

GOOD QUESTIONS PUMP LIFE INTO GOOD IDEAS
AND LET FLIMSY IDEAS QUIETLY DRIFT AWAY.

We covered a number of other core values in the course of the evening. About an hour later I said, "Get in groups and let's do a case study." When everyone was clustered I gave them a hypothetical situation that I had dreamed up just to test them. "Let's say that last Sunday someone in the church came up to you with an idea. She said, 'I was thinking that we should offer a vacation Bible school the week between Christmas and New Year's when the kids are off school. Kids have time on their hands and some parents have to work. We might reach a lot of kids.'" I asked my leaders, "What will you tell her?"

They talked a while and then I polled them. Without exception, each group proceeded to tell our hypothetical idea person all the reasons her idea would not work at our church. Some of the reasons were solid, but still I challenged them, "What happened to trying to say yes?"

I am not really suggesting that we agree to every idea. I mean that we lean toward a yes rather than a no. We explore and consider. A culture of grace recognizes that God has surprises up His sleeve. More than anyone else in the congregation, the pastor is situated to green-light God's surprises.

One way to distinguish off-the-cuff brainstorms from God-given burdens is to ask questions: *What made you think of that? Have you thought through some of the challenges? Have you talked about this idea with others? Is there some reason you think this would be especially effective at our church now? Are you invested in this idea enough to write up a short proposal I could show to others? Would you pray about this for a couple of weeks and see if God brings other people forward?* Good questions pump life into good ideas and let flimsy ideas quietly drift away.

After our meeting that night one fellow came up to me. "I heard about a church that did that very thing—that Christmas vacation Bible school idea," he said.

"You did? Somebody actually did that?" I replied in surprise.

"Yes," he said. "I heard that in about three years they had more kids coming that week than they got for their summer program." Why he didn't tell the whole group I'll never know.

Property Brothers

Pastors are sort of like property brothers with Jesus. We are on the lookout for congregational fixer-uppers. Once God points us to one of His local temples, we go to work with grace, the church's interior decorator, the ultimate renovation expert. When Wordworkers build into a church all the details and dimensions of God's grace in Christ, we build with gold, silver, and jewels that will only shine the brighter when the Day of Jesus dawns.

Chapter Seven

BUILDING WITH BROKEN PEOPLE

SAMUEL "SAMBO" Mockbee was a man on an architectural mission. His Rural Studio designed buildings for the
poor of Alabama that were architecturally creative and beautiful, but incredibly inexpensive to build and maintain. One of
his most famous buildings is Yancey Chapel, built on a wooded
ridge near Sawyerville, Alabama. The walls, curving in like
backwards parentheses, are made from a thousand worn-out
tires covered with stucco. The soaring ceiling beams were sal-
vaged from a house, and the rusty tin shingles came from old
local barns. The slate on the floor came from a creek bed. The
pulpit and font were made from scrap metal. Mockbee said of
his buildings, "Everyone, rich or poor, deserves a shelter for
the soul."

When God builds a church He does it much like that. Sal-
vage and salvation are a lot alike. A few years ago our elders
were thinking on Matthew 9:36, "When he saw the crowds,
he had compassion on them, because they were harassed and

helpless, like sheep without a shepherd." We decided to take a simple survey in our morning worship service. We asked people to write down a brief response to the question, "How do you feel 'harassed and helpless' in your life and/or walk with Christ?" Not everyone does feel that way, of course, but we were surprised and saddened by the wide range of burdens: "Depression." "Constant pressure of deadlines." "Relationship with my husband." "I've been struggling with some deeply rooted sins." "Financial debt." "My ability to parent." There were many more and almost no two were alike. And these were people who were *not* "sheep without a shepherd." These were believers. Jesus Himself is their shepherd. And so am I. These are the worn and broken people we build into a church.

The Care of Souls

When I left seminary I had no idea that the soul has its own inner spiritual anatomy, its own nerves and muscles, pulse and memory. I had thought a lot about church, but not so much about souls. I'm not the only one. John Bunyan, the pastor who taught us how pilgrims progress, wrote, "The soul is such a thing, so rich and valuable in its nature, that scarce one in twenty thousand counts of it as they should."

God's people usually hope pastors will help them solve their problems—money or marriage problems, kids or work problems. I don't think anyone in all my years has ever asked me to help them take stock of their soul. People with problems almost never say to their pastor, "I would like you to help me refine the gold of my faith through this trial." They ask us why bad things are happening. Most just want to know if there is anything they can do (or that I can do) to make it go away. If we tell them what to do, and give them a spiritual kick in the pants, they're likely to feel we've done our job. But if we did not treat their souls we have failed. It is easy to forget that *their* priorities may not be God's priorities. After all, God does a lot to maneuver people into the often painful positions where they finally listen to Him. That is where we come in. The word *psychologist* got its start with the Greek word *psychē*—soul. Pastors are soul-ologists. Our work is the care and cure of souls.

Benefits Package for the Soul

In Psalm 103:1–2 David tells his soul to sing: "Praise the Lord, O my soul; all my inmost being, praise his holy name. Praise the Lord, O my soul, and forget not all his benefits." These are the privileges of God's salvation for our souls, our inmost beings. This list of the five salvation benefits for the soul reminds me of one of those heart-healthy lists you see at the doctor's office:

- He forgives all your sins.
- He heals all your diseases.
- He redeems your life from the pit.
- He crowns you with love and compassion.
- He satisfies your desires with good things so that your youth is renewed like the eagle's.

These traits of the grace-blessed soul are interlaced but

not identical. Helping God's people lay hold of all these benefits is the work of soul care. I suspect that every need of the harassed and helpless heart is addressed by these five gifts of God's grace in Christ.

IT IS A SWEET PRIVILEGE OF PASTORAL
WORDWORKERS TO SPEAK GOD'S FORGIVENESS TO
PEOPLE WHO FIND IT ALMOST TOO GOOD TO BE TRUE.

"Praise the Lord, O my soul, . . . who forgives all your sins." Sin takes many forms—deliberate acts of rebellion, bent living, even unintended mistakes. Sin dries out souls, leaving parts of our inward lives hardened against God, as if the nerve endings were deadened and the muscles atrophied. Worse still, sin in us is a contagion—spreading spiritual toxins throughout our own lives and then infecting others. The remedy of grace, quite simply, is forgiveness.

It is a sweet privilege of pastoral Wordworkers to speak God's forgiveness to people who find it almost too good to be true. The resurrected Christ breathed on His disciples and said, "Receive the Holy Spirit. If you forgive anyone's sins, their sins are forgiven; if you do not forgive them, they are not forgiven" (John 20:22–23 NIV).

I sat in a hospital room with a grieving young woman.

She had lost her baby in a miscarriage. At one point she said, "I must have done something awful to deserve this."

After a few moments I said, "I suppose it is possible that you have done some awful things. I don't know. Maybe you have even done things to deserve this. But dear sister, you are a Christian. Jesus died for whatever you have done. I don't know why you have to go through this heartache but I know this: You are not paying for your sin. Jesus did that. God is not punishing you."

"Praise the Lord, O my soul, . . . who heals all your diseases." Diseases of the soul, I think, are different from sins. They spring from sins, of course, though not necessarily our own. They are those conditions in all of us that are not willful sins but are attitudes born of error, suffering, or someone else's sin that keep us from enjoying the promises and privileges that rightfully belong to a blood-bought child of God.

Take fear. I doubt there is any command in Scripture more common than "Do not fear." Yet fear is never on the Bible's lists of sins. Fear is fed by the wicked whispers of things like faithlessness and idolatry, so sin is close at hand. But I deal with a fair amount of fear myself and I know it is much more like an affliction than an idol.

A couple of weeks after I had preached on Psalm 103, I realized that one of the diseases of my own soul is fear of conflict and criticism. I readily confessed this to the Lord (then and now) as a sin and a weakness, but I also knew I needed God's healing. As I prayed about this, I got the idea to catalog and read all the Bible verses that tell us not to be afraid. I had heard it was the most common command in Scripture. I found about 120 such passages and printed them out. I discovered that it is medicine to simply read them. When I mentioned this in a sermon, people began asking me for my list. I compiled a little booklet called *Whistling in the Dark* that lists all those passages. We've given away scores of them because those Scriptures are like a spiritual wonder drug for fear and anxiety.

THERE IS A KIND OF INWARD LONELINESS WHEN
PEOPLE DON'T GRASP THE TENDERNESS
OF THE FATHER'S AFFECTION.

I read somewhere that in the days when tuberculosis was common, a doctor would shake hands with his right hand but with his left he would grasp the other person's elbow. It seemed like a simple gesture of friendship, but a skilled physician could feel inflammation in the elbow that might indicate TB. We do that with the people who come to see us. We unobtrusively feel for diseases of the soul and when we discern a debilitating fear or hurt we bring Jesus to that specific need.

Pastors feel for the inflammation of injured and diseased hearts. Almost every pastor knows the signs of anxiety, crushed spirits, loneliness, self-loathing, or a victim's anger.

The grace of Jesus speaks to all of these. Sometimes the message is "repent," but not often. More likely Jesus says, "Come to Me, and I will give you rest." Pastors help people hear Jesus' promise of healing.

"Praise the Lord, O my soul, . . . who redeems your life from the pit." Our sin got us thrown into death's prison. We were "dead men walking." You've seen those pictures of gaunt prisoners, arms chained to damp underground dungeon walls. Our souls were like that. Some of our people are much more aware of the dungeon they came from than others. Pastors sometimes stand side-by-side with Christian brothers and sisters and look back into the pits from whence they have been redeemed. The very memory of such places is traumatic, and the saints do not always quite grasp that they don't have to look over their shoulders for the pursuing hounds. They are not escapees. They are redeemed and free, pardoned prisoners.

I recently told the story of John Wesley's conversion in a sermon. I explained how, in spite of being a minister and a missionary, he knew he did not have "that faith whereby alone we are saved." Then I told of his conversion at the Aldersgate Street chapel when, as he put it, "I felt I did trust in Christ, Christ alone, for salvation; and an assurance was given me, that He had taken away my sins, even mine, and saved me from the law of sin and death." After the sermon we sang his great hymn, "And Can It Be." "My chains fell off, my heart was free," goes the song. "I rose, went forth, and followed thee."

In the foyer after the service, Doug stood apart, looking a little dazed. He had tears in his eyes when he told me, "I think

I get it. I think I get it." Later he posted on his Facebook page, "Seeing the light and casting off chains. Feels good."

"Praise the Lord, O my soul, . . . who crowns you with love and compassion." Many of God's people can believe that God *forgives* them far more easily than they can believe He *loves* them. Some were orphans for so long or were such fierce rebels against God that being loved is too big a leap for their stunted faith. There is a kind of inward loneliness when people don't grasp the tenderness of the Father's affection, let alone the passion of our Bridegroom's love. People can accept that there is love in God's forgiveness, but they cannot imagine that God delights in them, that He is fond of them.

SOME PREACHERS AND COUNSELORS
SEEM TO THINK THAT THE MAIN PART OF A PASTOR'S
JOB IS TELLING PEOPLE TO BEHAVE. I THINK IT IS
TELLING CHRISTIANS HOW RICH THEY ARE.

I don't know how many times I have walked a person in counseling through the story of the return of the prodigal son in Luke 15. I think verse 20 is the most moving verse in the Bible: "So he got up and went to his father. But while he was still a long way off, his father saw him and was filled with compassion for him; he ran to his son, threw his arms around

106

him and kissed him." That was more than any such son dared hope for, yet the father "crowned" him with a signet ring, shoes for his bleeding feet, and a feast to celebrate his dead son come back to life.

When I met Kathy she was more messed up than I imagined. Eventually she attempted suicide not once but twice. A counselor friend, Eileen, and I did all we could, as did others who loved her, but Eileen was finally forced to have Kathy committed to the state mental hospital.

When I phoned Kathy there I could hear people shouting and cursing in the background. She said it was terrible. She cried when she told me that almost all her things had been stolen. Then late one night she was listening to a radio tucked under her pillow. The Christian host spoke quietly of the love of God the Father and then played the old hymn, "The Love of God." There and then Kathy grasped the Father's love for her. She had trusted Christ before that, but she did not know till then that her Savior had "crowned her with love and compassion." She walked out of that institution three days later and despite a lifetime of crushing physical problems has never again felt such despair. More than thirty years have passed and Kathy still calls me regularly to talk about God's love.

"Praise the Lord, O my soul, . . . who satisfies your desires with good things so that your youth is renewed like the eagle's." Unregenerate souls, like children who have lost their parents, spend the rest of their lives trying to find what they're missing: security, the comforting love of mealtimes and bedtimes, knowing who you are and what your name is. There are no desires more heartbreaking or desperate than the desires of an orphaned soul. Orphaned souls age too quickly and seldom rest easy.

When the ancient Jews saw an eagle molt—shed its feathers and take on new ones—it seemed to them like the eagle was young again. That's what the psalmist was thinking of. When Jesus meets the desires of our hearts for love and safety, for meaning here and a home with Him forever, when He gives us a family in the church and help in our prayers—when He satisfies all these desires—we are renewed inwardly. It is as if we drink from a fountain of youth.

MOST OF THE TIME INSISTING ON
RIGHTEOUSNESS IS A QUIET, EARNEST BUSINESS
BETWEEN A SHEPHERD AND A SHEEP.

I met Frederica by accident. I was leaving a nursing home and an aide had parked her wheelchair near the elevators. As I stood waiting there, I was drawn in by her beaming smile, and we started chatting. She loved Jesus and we became friends. We'd sing songs together and have Bible memory contests. I would start a passage like Psalm 23 and stop suddenly to see if she could finish it. She would quote a line or two and then stop to test me. Then we'd laugh. So far as I could tell, she owned nothing. It seemed that almost no one visited her. Her body ached. Yet her soul was young. Psalm 92:14 says that the righteous "will still bear fruit in old age, they will stay fresh and green, proclaiming, 'The Lord is upright; he is my Rock, and there is no wickedness in him.'" That was the elderly, youthful Frederica.

Some preachers and counselors seem to think that the main part of a pastor's job is telling people to behave. I think it is telling Christians how rich they are. Sheep wander off because they think the grass is greener somewhere else. So Wordworkers like us go out to find them and bring them back to Jesus' green pastures and still waters. We tell them Jesus really does satisfy their soul's desires with good things and that coming home to the Father is like getting a new lease on life.

Pastors are physicians of the soul. We administer these remedies of our Redeemer and then join the saints in singing, "Praise the Lord, O my soul, and forget not all his benefits."

Grace Brings Out the Worst in People

Grace brings out the worst in people, like a poultice. A poultice is cloth covered in medicine and placed over a wound to draw out an infection. We all love to hear testimonies of God's grace. Pastors also hear pre-testimonies; we hear the terrible things that happened before Jesus saved someone. We hear how those things hang on sometimes to torment Christians. So we need poultices saturated with grace to draw out spiritual infections. Here are some I use.

Things take time. I have a clock in my office made from a wide, weathered piece of a snow fence. Next to the clock face I carved into the wood the words, "Things take time." It is a necessary reminder for all who care for souls.

A couple lost their only daughter to cancer. She was in her midtwenties, just married, and as lovely as a princess. One Sunday many months after her death I preached about God's encouragement. Her parents came through the line as I was shaking hands. The mother looked at me, angry I think, and just said, "It doesn't work." It shook me.

I don't know what I said. Now, from this distance, I hope I said very little. I hope I hugged them if they would let me. I hope I didn't feel I needed to defend God. "Things take time."

In one of my own most painful times, a dear friend shared a statement by Teilhard de Chardin. "Above all else," he wrote, "trust in the slow work of God." Pastors learn patience, standing there watching over the flock. Repentance can take a long time. Doubt can linger for years. Broken relationships can languish for decades. Sometimes grace accelerates so fast that it makes your head snap back, but God's grace is not always in a hurry. Grace, and the pastor who dispenses it, know how to wait.

Clean house. I think of pastoral work as helping people redecorate their souls to make God at home. In sermons, counseling, and conversations, we help them lug out the lies and the sins that have turned their souls into pigsties. We insist on it. We tell people in no uncertain terms to stop sinning. I have a little ministry motto: "Law reveals; grace heals." In all this talk of grace, I do not want anyone to think that good pastors are patsies. We know how to lay down the life-giving law of the Lord. We know and trust church discipline.

But most of the time insisting on righteousness is a quiet, earnest business between a shepherd and a sheep. We say things like:

What's this I hear about your anger getting out of control?

Why don't I see you in church anymore?

I believe you when you say you love him, but the Bible says you may not live together until you're married. It is sin. Your relationship with Jesus is suffering, and you know it. Plus this is a toxic way to love your boyfriend. It has to stop.

You may be within your rights, but what you are doing is destroying your own heart. Your resentment is so strong I can feel the poison when I listen to you.

THE GOOD THING ABOUT THE GOSPEL IS THAT CHRIST ROBS GUILT OF ITS IMMORTALITY.

I'll give you two pieces of advice about confronting sinners. First, be careful with your own anger. It is easier (and it feels safer) to be angry than tender. There are times when righteous indignation is the only right response, but not many. Model mercy. Be kind.

Second, be patient but don't give up. Repentance can be a tough decision. It can take time to come to one's senses. Stay close. I told a young woman once, "I am not going to keep hammering you about this sin, but do not ever think it will be okay. Do not mistake my patience for acceptance."

Once people clean out the junk, we can then help them bring in the furnishings of truth and Christlike virtues. We must pray with them and for them. We teach them to pray biblical truth into their lives. Prayer, I think, is how holy furniture is carried into the soul.

Separate guilt from regret. "I feel so terrible about what happened," people say. It isn't clear what that means. A person who says, "I'm so sorry," can mean "I'm sorry for what I did. Please forgive me." Or "I feel so sad that this happened. Accept my sympathy." I've learned that it helps people a great deal to know which they are dealing with.

A man told me about a terrible accident he was involved with when he was in his early teens. Someone else was hurt badly because my friend had not been as careful as he should have been. He didn't sin. He was just a careless kid. But for decades he had carried debilitating guilt. Regret was natural and painful. But Satan's accusing lie said he could never be forgiven.

Pastors carry two distinct medications for these wounds. On the one hand, we treat real "I-have-sinned-against-God-and-against-you" guilt. The good thing about the gospel is that Christ robs guilt of its immortality. A pastor walks the guilt-ridden through soul-scouring confession. Over time, guilt has a way of worming its way into every corner of a person's mind. We help people confess it all to the Lord and, if possible, to the others they have offended. We stand guard against the Accuser's efforts to pile on vague and unfounded indictments. Then we take our brother or sister to the cross of Christ and pray with them until the burden rolls off their back and into the waiting sepulcher. When they feel they must shoulder it again, we stop them.

Regret is not so readily dispatched. Regret, I'm afraid, goes with this territory. I don't think it is likely that my friend will ever stop regretting the accident of that terrible day. Regret is the inevitable consequence of limping and lurching through this dark and heartbreaking world. The thing is, when the infection of guilt is removed, regret in the hands of the Lord becomes a sanctifying influence. It can shape saints instead of just crushing them.

Plunder the old captors. When God delivered Israel out of Egypt He told them to ask the Egyptians "for articles of silver and gold and for clothing." And the Egyptians "gave them what they asked for; so they plundered the Egyptians" (Exodus 12:35–36). I tell people to plunder their past bondage for treasures they can give to God. For example, I watched godly women who had been sexually abused as children build a wise and effective ministry to other victims. I saw a widow still grieving reach out to help another woman who had just lost her husband. They plundered their pasts to build the Body of Christ. In Exodus, when Israel brought all kinds of precious metals, jewels, and fabrics to build God's Tabernacle, I assume those treasures were what they had plundered from their former taskmasters. Pastors give people the courage and faith to plunder their past sorrows and slavery for treasure. Then God takes those former slaves and their treasures to build us into His temple.

Chapter Eight

MARCH INTO
THE SMOKE

I HAD NEVER been so overwhelmed by a church situation. When I accepted the call to this church I knew things had been bad. I knew things were still bad. So I came with my eyes open. But I never reckoned on how bad it would *feel*.

It would not be prudent to tell you all that had transpired before I arrived in February 1998, but here is what I came to.

To begin with, none of the six elders who had called me to this position three months before were still in those positions when I arrived. Only two were still in the church and one of those was leaving within six weeks. They were good men and I'm not criticizing them. But it was a hard way to start. Consequently, the church had only been able to find three candidates to stand for elder at the election two weeks before I started. Even that had blown up. On my first Sunday, the evening prayer service I planned turned into an unpleasant conflict over whether two of those men had been rightfully elected. (They had.)

Two weeks after I started, we had our first Elder Board meeting. Our chair told us that at current rates of spending the church was about six weeks from bankruptcy. My family's moving expenses had not been paid yet and we had just signed a contract on our house. What was going to happen to us?

One strange discovery I made when I started was that virtually all the file cabinets of the church had been emptied. Who did that and why I'm not certain, but we had no board minutes, reports, photos, and almost no records. We were like a church with amnesia. Gradually I learned that the church had enjoyed times of great blessing. I also heard terrible things.

THE HARD PART OF PRAYING THAT NIGHT
WASN'T PRAYING FOR THE CHURCH.
IT WAS WHAT LAY BURIED IN ME.

By the time I came the church was not so much divided as it was shell-shocked. It reminded me of those war-ruined cities where bridges are gone, the power and water supplies are gone, and people are scared to come out of their bunkers.

The church prayed. Our chairman skillfully found ways to help us get our finances stabilized. A few more people drifted out, but most folks started to settle in. I preached through 1 John so we would remember how important it is to love one another as believers.

I decided to preach next from Joshua. I felt the most important sermon would be on chapter 7, about the hidden sin of Achan that sabotaged Israel's success. There had been a rather long history of difficulties in the church, and I wondered often if spiritual toxic waste below the surface of our life together was poisoning us in ways we couldn't see. I decided that this would be a kind of line-in-the-sand sermon. I asked God to make clear if there was "sin in the camp" so we could either address it or move on. I prayed a great deal as that Sunday approached. I decided I would do something I had never done before (or since). I stayed at church all Saturday night, praying as long as I could.

The hard part of praying that night wasn't praying for the church. It was what lay buried in me. When I left my previous congregation, unknown to most, I carried some deep resentment. That Saturday night as I prayed, I was afraid I might be the Achan. I was ready to do whatever I needed to do to set things right.

I assumed that God would require me to talk to people—especially one person—who had frustrated me deeply. The problem was that this person had no idea how difficult he had been for me. To confess my sin to him would actually burden him with a kind of condemnation he didn't need. ("I'm sorry that I have resented you so much for what you did to me.") That night God impressed on me what He wanted me to do, something I had never thought of before. First, I honestly repented to God for this festering frustration. Then the Spirit told me, "You do not need to call him, but every time you think of him"—and I thought of him a lot!—"I want you to bless him. Pray for him. Ask God to delight him." So that is what I began to do that very night. Within a couple of weeks I was released from the headlock of my resentment and my unsuspecting brother was blessed many, many times.

The next morning I concluded my sermon on Joshua 7 with a sober call to repentance. I don't know what happened in people's hearts, but I went home confident that after that morning we stood before God with clean hands. The past was almost behind us.

EVERY BELIEVER HAS BIBLICAL ALTARS WHERE
WE HAVE MET GOD IN PAST STRUGGLES.

We had addressed the issue of hidden sin, but our elders and I realized we also had to deal with the harm that had been done to particular people. One evening my wife and I had several couples to our home who had all spent time in exile from the church and had returned. These were strong and mature believers. I expected to ask them how they were doing, hear how they'd put the painful past behind them, tell them how glad we were to have them back, and then we'd all have some dessert. Instead we heard three hours of heartbreak. Later my wife and I heard other sad stories from some of the young people. Almost every time we were with people we heard hurts. Somehow we had to deal with that.

Most of the healing came quietly and gradually through the Spirit's ministry among us. But the elders and I felt we needed to take a public step. As we approached our annual congregational meeting near the end of my first year, we had an idea. At our meeting, after we had dealt with other business, I stood to address the members. "Some of you have been hurt badly in this church," I began. "Things have been said and done here that should have never happened. The problem is that those who should apologize are no longer here." I pointed to specific people and said to each of them, "On behalf of the elders I want to say we're sorry." I think the great weight upon our little congregation lifted that night.

BE BRAVE

Years ago my friend David, knowing I like Civil War history, gave me a coffee mug with a painting on it by Mort Künstler entitled, "Steady, Boys, Steady." It portrays one brigade of Pickett's Charge, the ill-fated bloodbath that was part of the Battle of Gettysburg on July 3, 1863. The painting shows a long double line of ragtag Confederate soldiers, bayoneted guns resting on their shoulders, marching forward. One man carries their flag. Everything around them is obscured by the smoke of cannons and there are explosions nearby. Out ahead of them, the focal point of the picture, is Brigade Commander Lewis Armistead. He is perhaps ten feet ahead of his troops. His hat is raised high on the tip of his saber so his troops can see to follow.

In those first frightening months in this church I looked at the picture on that coffee mug at least a hundred times. I'd look at Lewis Armistead and think, *He must have been frightened, too. But when you are a leader, sometimes you just put your hat on your sword and march into the smoke.* Over and over I'd tell myself, *Put your hat on your sword and march into the smoke.*

The way pastors deal with the turmoil around us depends on how we deal with the turmoil within us. I used to teach a seminary class where students would bring in real-life case studies and we would talk through how to handle them. The students were always so reasonable and analytical about these dilemmas, so I started asking, "What would this problem likely do to you inwardly? How would you handle something like this emotionally?" What happens within us during harrowing times affects the outcome of the story. Surely Lewis Armistead marched into the smoke so bravely because of how he had been shaped inwardly. I read recently that Armistead, who died two days after that battle, had written in the cover of his prayer book, "Trust God and fear nothing." Easier said than done.

I'm a coward at heart; so for me, at least, courage requires a healthy infusion of God's grace. Messes frighten me deeply. I hate to "march into the smoke." I have learned that God uses these surprising tools to sculpt a brave heart.

OUR SOULS NEED TRUTH

Like soldiers confused by the smoke and din of battle, our souls can become disoriented by conflict, loss, attacks, and pain. They cause a kind of battlefield panic. We cannot think straight. When that happens to pastors, we become a danger to the congregation following us. A lot of people can get hurt if we don't have our wits about us. Pastors whose souls are tangled in lies make terrible shepherds.

When the battlefield smoke is thick, take great gulps of Scripture to clear your head. There is hardly anything more basic, but we forget when we're frightened. Scripture takes us aloft to see what is really going on from God's perspective and takes us within to see the good and bad truth about our own hearts.

Every believer has biblical altars where we have met God in past struggles. Next to Psalm 16 in my Bible I have written "2/98," that first tumultuous month in this church. "Keep me safe, O God," I prayed often, taking my cue from the psalm, "for in you I take refuge. . . . Apart from you I have no good thing." That passage also reminded me that God loved His people, "the glorious ones in whom is all my delight," and that despite the frightening circumstances, I was well situated: "Lord, you have assigned me my portion and my cup; you have made my lot secure. The boundary lines have fallen for me in pleasant places; surely I have a delightful inheritance." I needed to pray those words in order to remember that things are not always what they seem.

Next to Acts 18:9–11 in my Bible I have written "8/91." When I went back and read my journal it was obvious what a tough month it had been. I was anxious about a troubling letter I had received. I was discouraged by my sins. A woman in the congregation was angry with me, rightfully, because I had responded so slowly to a crisis in her marriage. A family told me they were leaving the church. I had to do a funeral for a thirty-six-year-old woman, and on the way home from the funeral I visited Jim, our beloved candy man I wrote about earlier, who was dying of cancer. You can see why it seemed like God was talking directly to me when I read in Acts 18:9–10, "One night the Lord spoke to Paul in a vision: 'Do not be afraid; keep on speaking, do not be silent. For I am with you, and no one is going to attack and harm you, because I have many people in this city.' So Paul stayed for a year and a half, teaching them the word of God." It turns out He had many people in our town, too.

DO NOT GO SOUR

I've never forgotten the title of a *Leadership* journal article in 2000: "Why Am I Angrier Than I Used to Be?" We all have our reasons and our stories. Frustration is an occupational hazard going back to Moses.

When I was sixteen, I worked in a tiny grocery store in my hometown. We kept a quart of milk in the big walk-in cooler and a couple of us would slip in and take a swig on hot days, straight from the carton. One August afternoon I went in and guzzled milk like a camel at an oasis. It took a couple of seconds before I tasted it. It had gone terribly sour. I gagged and dashed for the back door. That's what it is like for a congregation whose pastor has gone sour.

Ed came to see me a couple of years ago. He was an elder and a friend from church. He is also a professional counselor with many years of experience. He had obviously thought and prayed about what he wanted to say to me. After some small talk he got to the point. "You are depressed and you are angry," he said, "and you need to find out why." I don't think many people in church would have guessed that, but he was right. I was embarrassed and relieved at the same time. I hated the pressure that was building inside me. Thankfully, God provided a skilled counselor to help me get my balance, because a sour pastor can make a whole church sick.

THERE IS A DIRECT LINK BETWEEN SPIRITUAL
COURAGE AND HUMILITY. THE LINK IS LOVE.

Ed had something else to say to me that day, and it didn't land as well. It isn't important for anyone else to know all the details, but suffice it to say he has long wanted me to change something about the way I preach, and preaching is my pride and joy. Partly, I disagree with him. Partly, after years of trying, I just can't do what he (and some others) want me to do. That afternoon I felt both threatened and helpless. He was as nice as he could be, but we just don't see eye to eye on this and I was fed up with it. I suppose part of my reaction was due to the anger and depression that were already wreaking havoc in my soul. Still, I felt hurt and put-upon. I wanted him to just leave me alone, and I kept him at arm's length in the months that followed.

About six months later we were planning a worship service focusing on how Jesus serves us. In our brainstorming meeting we had an idea: "Why don't we have someone wash someone else's feet?" I volunteered to make the arrangements.

I started by looking for a volunteer foot washer. And guess what? I could not find a single person who was available. I probably made ten calls and no one could do it. Time was running out, so I did what pastors often do. I decided to take care of it myself. *I can wash feet,* I thought. *I'm certainly not too proud to do that.*

The next question was whose feet should I wash. Only one name came to mind: Ed. *No! I don't want to do that!* I protested to the Spirit. But it was like God wiped out all the other names in our church directory. So finally, reluctantly, I called Ed.

He knew what this meant to our relationship before I told him. He was gracious to me. So that Sunday morning, while someone sang Michael Card's "The Basin and the Towel," I brought Ed to the chair on the platform. I took off his shoes and socks and humbled myself to the place where I should have been all along. Most people that morning did not realize what they were seeing, but I will not forget it. I got low enough to let Ed back in. Forgiveness wasn't the issue. Neither of us needed that. For me, it was about vulnerability. The older I get the more guarded I am. I think that is true for most pastors. This can be a bruising business, and if we can keep tying pillows around us we don't feel people's punches. Of course, we can't feel touches of love very well either.

There is a kind of relief in the humility of washing feet, and now things with Ed and me are where they should be. There is a direct link between spiritual courage and humility. The link is love.

Pastors are often credited publicly for being more saintly than we really are. I get jittery when someone prays, "Thank You, Lord, for the godly pastor You've given us." Thus, it is only fitting that when it comes to our faults we sometimes have to take our medicine publicly.

SHARING IN THE SUFFERINGS OF CHRIST

"Sharing in the sufferings of Christ" is a phrase that makes many of us uneasy, because we're not sure we do it. We feel a little sheepish putting ourselves in the same category as martyrs. But all growing Christians share in Christ's sufferings. We don't have a choice about it. Essentially this means that we accept the shame and disgrace of the crucified life for Christ's sake. All that the Lord produces in our lives and all we are taught in Scripture runs headlong into the ways of the world around us, and the world pushes back. Pastors share this Christlike suffering with all believers. Indeed, a great part of our work is helping our fellow believers understand how they share in the sufferings of Christ.

In one sense, Christ's suffering continues now in the suffering of His Body, the church. For example, the cries of the martyrs waiting for justice under the altar (Revelation 6:9–10) surely grieve the Lord. Jesus suffers when there is strife in His Body among his people. As Christ's under-shepherds we bear with Him the sufferings of the church. In that sense, there are ways that pastoral suffering is uniquely Christlike.

For one thing, we carry the spiritual weight of a whole congregation. Pastors identify with Paul in 2 Corinthians 11:29, "Who is weak, and I do not feel weak? Who is led into sin, and I do not inwardly burn?" Jesus feels that way about His church, too. A friend told me once what a spiritual weight lifted from his shoulders when his term as elder concluded. Pastors almost never get out from under that burden.

Like Paul, we pastors feel the weakness of our people. They are so fragile sometimes. One morning I stood at the bedside of an utterly incapacitated woman and I could not even read Scripture because of my tears. I remember sitting with a brother who had just sabotaged his whole life and I felt sick with the pain of it all. Once a man matter-of-factly told me a terrible, sordid story from his childhood.

"Brother," I blurted out, "that's child abuse."

He stopped cold while my words worked their way into his mind. Then he began to sob harder than I have ever seen anyone cry anywhere. I hugged him, and I cried too. With Jesus, we suffer the griefs of all these aching people.

Then there are the effects of sin within the church. Sin in our churches fires a painful indignation in pastors who are jealous for holiness. It hurts Jesus and it hurts us. What's more, we can also get hurt by it.

I had been a solo pastor less than a year when I got a call about nine o'clock in the evening from a distraught husband.

He and his wife had had a big fight and she had kicked him out. He didn't know how to stand up to her and he didn't know where to go. I covered the phone and whispered the story to my wife. We agreed to take him in for the night. He was relieved but told me he had to go back home to get clothes for work the next day. I said I would go with him.

SHARING IN THE SUFFERINGS OF CHRIST HURTS.
BUT IT ALSO MAKES US MORE LIKE JESUS.

When we walked in the front door his wife unloaded. She raged while we went to the bedroom closet. She turned her anger on me. It felt like a boxer's body blows. I started talking her down. Three hours later I left them together, smiling. A good night's work for a pastor.

But something went wrong in me that night. Some vital emotional organ had been bruised. Within a day or two I plunged into a deep depression. I was afraid of the phone and the dark. I couldn't watch a TV drama. All I wanted to do was sleep. I had no sense whatever of God's presence. I clung to the advice I had heard, "Never doubt in the darkness what you knew to be true in the light." I told a few of my leaders what was happening to me and they prayed for me.

About two weeks later I read something about Jesus

healing memories. There is dangerous nonsense out there on that subject. But what I read simply recommended inviting Jesus to come into a bad memory. Don't try to visualize Him or imagine what He would do. Just pray and ask Jesus to bring His healing. It wasn't hard to bring that scene back to my mind. There she was, yelling on one side of the bed and on the other side, while her husband nervously grabbed things from the closet, I was trying to calm her. I realized as I prayed that I was very angry with Jesus. "Where were You?" I cried. "I just stood there and took all that venom, and where were You, Jesus?"

I don't know how He spoke, but I was not expecting what I heard: "I was right there beside you." I still feel the medicine in that story every time I tell it. Of course He was. That is what it is like sometimes to serve Christ. Why didn't I know that? Do you know what else He said? He said, "You did well." He really said that.

Sharing in the sufferings of Christ hurts. But it also makes us more like Jesus.

WHEN THE SMOKE CLEARS

Pastoral courage does not only come from battlefield experience. It comes from that hard, lonely interior work that God does on our souls.

Recently my young friend Tony called me. He is a pastor, too. When I asked how he was, he said, "I'm not doing so well. Do you have a few minutes to talk?" My heart sank. I braced myself for bad news.

He told me that one of his elders had died suddenly and

he had to do the funeral in a couple of days. On his way to the elder's home his car broke down. His wife, Julie, was eight months pregnant and there were some concerns about that. They had just closed on a house and discovered scores of dead mice behind the basement walls. Even the good news was bad. The church was growing so quickly he didn't know how they could accommodate people and the responsibility was weighing him down. In short, he was overwhelmed.

"Oh, Tony," I said, "when I heard your voice I was afraid you were going to tell me you had failed Jesus, but you have been faithful! I know this is a terribly hard time, but what a good pastor you are! Jesus is pleased." We talked through the various things he had mentioned and prayed together. When I checked on him a few weeks later, the smoke had cleared. He wrote, "Both cars are running, mice are gone, walls are up, the funeral lifted Jesus high, baby and mom are healthy, and I am in awe of God's grace."

Pastors have to be brave. That day as we talked I should have told Tony the story about the picture on my coffee cup. He was learning, as I have, that sometimes all you can do is put your hat on your sword and march into the smoke.

Chapter Nine

"I'D HAVE
WAITED ALL NIGHT"

GRACE FEEDS on grace. If pastors are to dispense grace every time we turn around, then we need to take in grace the way runners take in carbs before a marathon. Jesus is our manna, our living grace, the bread of heaven. When we don't get enough of Christ we get spiritually lightheaded and weak in the knees. What's worse than weakness is that pastors who are not nourished by Christ's grace get crotchety, indifferent, or suspicious around God's people. We take on a Pharisee scowl every time people don't perform. Our flocks stop seeing Jesus through us. Our Wordwork takes on a loveless clanging.

Like all believers, pastors are nourished by Christ when we come to sit, like Mary did, at His feet. Christ nourishes us when we study the Scriptures and when we pray for strength and wisdom. He feeds us when we worship and come to the Lord's table, and when we overhear our own sermons and lessons as we speak them.

Ironically, pastors tend to overlook one of the most

fundamental ways the Lord Jesus nourishes us with grace: through the very church we serve. It is His Body, after all. The church feeds us as surely as we feed the church. Communion not only preaches Jesus' shed blood but also the nourishment His Body provides for us, His Body the church. First Corinthians 10:16–17 says, "And is not the bread that we break a participation in the body of Christ? Because there is one loaf, we, who are many, are one body, for we all partake of the one loaf."

A PASTOR WHO DOESN'T LEARN SUBMISSION
WILL DRIVE SHEEP RATHER THAN LEAD THEM.

All believers are nourished through Jesus' church. But pastors often enjoy graces that few others will experience. When we forget this, we are like hungry people passing the pantry oblivious to what we're missing. Sadly, some pastors serve churches that are about as nourishing as Styrofoam, but most congregations feed their pastors.

THE GRACE OF SUBMISSION

Being both headstrong and defensive, I have wished more than once that God wasn't so big on submission. Yet Jesus has persistently used His church to give me this gift. A pastor who doesn't learn submission will drive sheep rather than lead them.

Submission is a gift that often comes dressed in grave-digger's clothes. It is easy, of course, to submit to a senior pastor, board, or congregation that sees things the way we do. But submitting is a killer when we feel sure they are wrong and we're paying the price.

I was still a rookie pastor when I attended my first Walk Thru the Bible seminar. It was the most innovative way of teaching the Bible I had ever seen, and I wanted in. I applied and was stunned when a man called to say he wanted to fly to Chicago to interview me. Next thing I knew I was offered the opportunity to teach. Most of the other teachers were pastors or professors who flew to a destination on a Friday evening, taught all day Saturday, and then were home in time for church on Sunday. Perfect. I wouldn't have to give up a thing. There was just one small thing: Walk Thru the Bible required me to get the church board's permission.

They didn't give it to me, and they never really told me why. They just said no. I was shocked, angry, and deeply disappointed. A friend on the board said some of the leaders were worried that another church would "steal" me. That really ticked me off!

Some four months later I was frantic with all the work of a full-time ministry plus part-time seminary. I was hurrying to a class one Thursday when, out of the blue, the Lord seemed to whisper, "So what if you were flying somewhere to teach for Walk Thru the Bible this weekend on top of everything else?" I realized instantly that something would have had to go; probably my education, and that would have been a terrible mistake. I thought about how angry I had been with my church's leaders. That is when I learned that, apart from matters of deepest biblical conviction, God expects us to submit to those over us whether or not they make sense. Submission is a grace because God uses it to protect us, direct us, and sanctify us, even when we don't want help.

Submission is also a grace-gift because it practically forces humility on us, and that is about the only way some of us will come to it.

One evening a long time ago I stood in the back of the auditorium as the congregational vote was finally reported. I thought the proposal I'd brought to the church was a no-brainer; actually I thought it was a gift from God. But there had been a lot of suspicion—of me, I think, more than the proposal. Some people felt pushed and probably thought I was throwing my weight around once too often. The motion needed a 75 percent approval. It got 72 percent. I couldn't believe it. I stood there in the back and, for the first time, thought seriously about leaving the church. To make matters worse, there was a new members' class waiting for me in another room. I wasn't in the mood to tell new people how great our church was.

Submitting to that decision came slowly. Someone afterward said, "It must have been God's will." But God's people have often done things that didn't please God. I finally concluded that I might never actually know what God's will was in this matter. But I also gradually realized that it *was* God's will for me to submit to that decision, right or wrong, because

God wanted me to face three issues. 1) Some in the church no longer trusted me. 2) I had not been fair to people in rushing them through the process of decision making. 3) God would work for the good of all who trusted Him in this, whatever their vote, and is gracious enough to bless His church even if the decision was wrong.

THE GRACE OF THE FRONT ROW SEAT

This side of the cloud of witnesses, pastors have the best seat in the house for seeing God work among His people. I cannot think of another job on earth in which someone sees and hears what a pastor does. Much of what we witness feeds our souls. We grow in faith, hope, and love because we sit so close to the action.

For example, pastors midwife new births more often than most other Christians. We're told to seek the lost, but sometimes the lost seek us. Let me tell you just one story. Dan and I became acquainted through a wedding I performed. He was a strange combination of skeptical scientist and street fighter. He was brilliant, combative, uncontrolled, and as arrogant as Nebuchadnezzar. Dan didn't just consider the Lord, he sparred with Him. Finally, one day he came down to his last gasp. "I don't think I can live up to being a good Christian," he said. "I'm sure you can't," I replied, and talked to him about grace and the working of the Holy Spirit. The fight went out of him and he was ready for Jesus.

"Dan, you are a very proud man," I said. "I've never asked anyone to do this before, but when you ask Jesus into your heart, I think you should do it on your knees. You need to remember that you bowed before Him as Lord." So Dan knelt for maybe the first time in his life and gladly became a subject of the King. Only a couple of years later at age thirty-six, Dan's heart gave out, and this was the story I told at his funeral. The grace of Christ that saved Dan fed me for a long time.

From our front row seats, pastors are sometimes close enough to see God's grace in battle gear, coming to the aid of a saint like one of those "mighty men" around David. Kathleen was a delightful and effective Christian, but she was tormented by a dark, demonic power within who relentlessly urged her toward terrible fear and destructiveness. My associate pastor, Freddy, and his wife Eileen had considerable experience in spiritual warfare, so my wife and I went with them to meet with Kathleen and her husband in their apartment.

FROM MY PLACE IN THE FRONT ROW I SEE QUIET AND ASTONISHING GENEROSITY, DOGGED DAILY SERVICE, AND LOVE BLANKETING A MULTITUDE OF SINS.

Under Freddy's guidance, Kathleen drew on the strong name of Jesus first to identify the spirit tormenting her. A name came to her clearly, which she recognized as the name of one of the false gods mentioned in the Old Testament. Kathleen mentioned that she spoke in a tongue, so Freddy asked her to do so. Again, invoking the name of the Lord Jesus Christ, she insisted the spirit translate what he was saying. After a moment of quiet she looked up, shocked, "He's saying, 'I hate you! I hate you! I hate you!'" Freddy instructed her in her invincible position in Christ and her right as a child of God to demand that the spirit leave her. We prayed with her as she prayed aloud that Jesus Christ would banish the demon and reign completely in her life. We all grew quiet for a few moments. Then Kathleen raised her head, eyes shining, and said simply, "They're gone."

Not many Christians see something like that. You cannot imagine how many times that story has fed my confidence in the strong name of Christ.

From my place in the front row I see quiet and astonishing generosity, dogged daily service, and love blanketing a multitude of sins. I watch through the dark shadows as brothers and sisters wrestle with the Lord until they limp into the light. I've watched saints straighten their shoulders and go out to face death. Again and again, I have seen God's people trust Him and I've only rarely seen people turn away. "Didn't you ever get angry with God?" I asked a friend who had suffered a crushing loss. "No, I never did," he said. "I grieved, but I knew God was good." Remember how Jesus' disciples picked up whole baskets of food left over when Jesus fed the five thousand? Pastors do that, too.

THE GRACE BEHIND THE NUMBERS

Pastors are notoriously preoccupied with numbers. Sunday's attendance. Last month's giving. How many people signed up for the dinner or seminar. We keep telling ourselves and each other that numbers aren't what matter, but it is a tough sell! Regardless of whether they are going up or down, numbers are untrustworthy counselors. Yet the grace of God is in those numbers if you know how to decode it.

OFFERING ENVELOPES DON'T JUST CARRY CHECKS. THEY ALSO CARRY FAITH AND SACRIFICE FOR JESUS' SAKE. PEOPLE PUT PRAISE IN AN OFFERING PLATE AND WE DON'T HEAR A SOUND.

The numbers tell me that we had five visitors. The encoded message of grace is that two of them, from a country on the other side of the world, have never come to church before. Two others are out-of-town parents thrilled to see that their daughter is attending such a good church. And as for the fifth, Jeff, who rarely shows up himself, brought a buddy he used to work with.

When our ushers count our attendance, they stand at the back of the auditorium and count the backs of heads. Pastors had better know the faces. Over there is a couple who may not yet be Christians. Their former neighbors have prayed for them for years, and now here they are. Toward the back left side there is a row of some of the church's grandmothers.

They will go out for lunch together after the service and then visit one of their group who can't get out to church any more. There is a young man who told me he loves reading A. W. Tozer. Over there, a young woman who wants to be a missionary in Europe. There in the back is a woman who has started a blog about being a servant of Christ in a secular workplace. There is the couple grieving the loss of a son and the terrible illness of a daughter-in-law, and yet they sing.

Whether there are more people here this week than last doesn't matter so much when you look at the faces.

Finances work the same way. Offering envelopes don't just carry checks. They also carry faith and sacrifice for Jesus' sake. People put praise in an offering plate and we don't hear a sound. Jesus asked in Luke 16:11, "If you have not been trustworthy in handling worldly wealth, who will trust you with true riches?" There are many in our churches who *are* trustworthy and whom God *has* trusted with true riches, and we are their pastors.

Recently we invited the Gideons to make a presentation in our service, and we took a special offering for them. When it was counted, the man who made the presentation wept for joy. The next Sunday when we told the congregation that our gifts would purchase more than 340 Bibles, we all applauded the grace of God at work among us.

THE GRACE OF THE LONG HAUL

Pastoral work is slow going most of the time. There are moments of high drama, to be sure, but mostly we watch sheep grow. One of God's gracious gifts to pastors, if you stick with it awhile, is seeing the slow, inexorable work of His grace in lives and in a church.

Matt was my first child dedication, some thirty years ago now. I wrote earlier that since I started carrying babies through the congregation for their blessing I had never had one cry. But that first time, the little guy went berserk there on the platform in front of God and everybody. Screamed and twisted so that all I could do was put my hand on his head and try to pray loudly enough to be heard over his bawling. His life has been kind of like that, from what his parents tell me. But the good work God began that day is far closer to completion. Matt, who wandered far, has come home from the far country, married a wonderful Christian woman, and despite dropping out of high school, now has a masters degree. The baby who didn't want to be dedicated to Christ is now His growing disciple and father of two little ones of his own.

In the summer of 2004, I heard that our former church baptized thirty-five people out at the lake. One of them was Harold. I could hardly believe it. Linda, Harold's wife, had prayed for him for thirty years. He had always been a great guy—kind, helpful, very willing to let Linda and the boys be involved in church—but he just wasn't interested. He had even invited me to be the chaplain for his volunteer fire department. When I heard about the baptism, I called them to get the story straight. "Harold," I said, "what's this I hear?"

He said that some tough times were getting the best of him a few months earlier. He asked Linda to go with him to see the pastor. In the course of that meeting, Pastor Jeff asked

Harold if he would like to accept Christ. Harold said yes. Linda said she was shocked. She told me on the phone, "I waited all those years to have him sit beside me in church." She said that when Harold was baptized, through his tears, he thanked everyone for praying all those years. "He's ushering at church," she told me. "You've never seen anyone so proud to be an usher." I know everyone in the church rejoiced over the grace in that story, but I suspect Pastor Jeff and I fed on it as only pastors can.

One evening a few years ago, Cathy called me. When I first met her, some twenty years earlier, she was recovering from a divorce and trying to set her life right with the Lord. She told me about her profoundly mentally handicapped son, Nicholas. He was in a care facility nearby and she would visit him every week.

When Nicholas was eight or nine years old Cathy came to me with an unusual request. She asked if the elders of our church would anoint and pray for Nicholas in keeping with James 5:14–16. Cathy said she wasn't thinking that God might heal all Nicholas's disabilities; she simply felt that God wanted her to have the elders pray for him. She didn't know why. So one Sunday she brought him to church in a wheelchair and after the service we met in my office, anointed Nicholas with oil, and prayed for him.

Nicholas was twenty-five years old when Cathy called me all those years later. Every week for twenty-five years Cathy had visited him. In all those visits Nicholas never communicated with her except for laughing sometimes as she entered the room. It seemed that nothing ever changed.

Cathy had just had her annual consultation with the team of professionals who care for Nicholas. In the course of that meeting the speech therapist said, "I think Nicholas is making some progress. We've been using green and red cards for 'yes' and 'no.' He is learning to point at the right card in answer to some questions. Would you like to see?"

"Of course," Cathy replied, her heart pounding. So they went to Nicholas's room.

The therapist held up the green and red cards, and asked, "Nicholas, is your mom with us today?" And Nicholas pointed at the green card. Cathy could hardly believe it. Other questions convinced her that it wasn't an accident; he really understood.

She called me in tears to tell me her good news. "All these years I'd visit him," she said, "and I never knew if he even knew who I was. And now I know. He knows I'm his mother. And he is excited to see me." Then Cathy asked, "Do you remember when the elders prayed for Nicholas? This is God's answer." Guess what I think about now when someone asks our elders to pray for them?

THE GRACE OF UPHELD HANDS

Exodus 17 tells how Joshua led the Israelites into battle while Moses, Aaron, and Hur watched from a high hill. Verses 11–13 say:

> As long as Moses held up his hands, the Israelites were winning, but whenever he lowered his hands, the Amalekites were winning. When Moses' hands grew tired, they took a stone and put it under him and he sat on it. Aaron and Hur held his hands up—one on one side, one on the other—so

that his hands remained steady till sunset. So Joshua overcame the Amalekite army with the sword.

Like many other pastors, I have known the descendants of Aaron and Hur. I have felt the grace of their hands lifting mine.

In the frightening early days in this church, I was deeply disheartened to see people leave who had warmly welcomed us only three months before. I hadn't even had time to mess up! One day Dill happened by my office. She is as stalwart a soul as I know, and like a mother to me. I told her of my discouragement. "Lee," she said, "if everyone else leaves, I will follow you out the door and turn off the lights." What a gracious gift of God to have someone hold up your weary hands until the battle turns.

One night years ago, a couple demanded a meeting with me and another person with whom they were very upset. They also insisted on having an elder present and another couple for their support. They had gone through a painful loss and I felt then (and now) that I had done a good job making sure they were cared for by the church and a counselor. They were hurt and angry that I personally hadn't done more. I don't think I have ever taken such a tongue lashing, and I had to take it with witnesses.

A few days earlier someone had given me one of those little WWJD bracelets, and it was still sitting on my desk. I kept glancing at it while they scolded me. What would Jesus do? The only verse the Lord brought to my mind was 1 Peter 2:23, "When they hurled their insults at him, he did not retaliate."

These people who were so angry with me were in no way like Jesus' enemies. In fact, they were His beloved children. I am by nature incredibly defensive, but I knew I had to be silent even as Jesus had been. So I sat there saying almost nothing, feeling like a punching bag. When they were finished I was wrung out. But the evening wasn't over. I'm a pastor so, naturally, I had a committee meeting waiting for me.

It was about 9:30 p.m. when everyone left. I was bone-tired and shaken. As I walked out of my office into the dark foyer I noticed a light on in the church library. I went to shut it off and found Tom there. "What are you doing here?" I asked.

"I heard you had kind of a rough meeting," he said.

"Yeah, it was," I agreed. Tears came to my eyes. When I regained my composure I asked, "Have you been waiting all this time? How did you know how long I'd be?"

"I didn't," Tom said, "but I would have waited here all night to be sure you were all right." And he hugged me.

There are times when pastors have to go it alone, but thank God for the times He sends us the heirs of Aaron and Hur.

Chapter Ten

"LEAD ME GENTLY HOME"

THE LAST TIME I saw either Marie or Lars was an after-noon in early December. They were both in their nineties and both very near death. They had never met and, sadly, they never ever would.

Marie was ninty-two and a saint if ever there was one. Every Sunday she'd come up to me after the service. "Oh Pastor!" she would say, clasping my hand, "Thank you for that message! It was *such* a blessing!" It had been some months since Marie had been in church. She was growing weaker and weaker and was aching for heaven. Sometimes she would ask, "Why am I here? I just want to go home."

I found her that afternoon in a four-bed ward in the nurs-ing home. She was so tiny and frail I didn't recognize her at first. She smiled faintly when I sat down on the edge of her bed. She could barely speak. I held her hand, leaned down, and said, "Marie, it won't be long now. You'll soon be going home to be with Jesus." She smiled that heart-melting smile and whispered, "Great! Great! Great!"

PASTORS WALK PEOPLE TO THE EDGE OF
THE WORLD AND WATCH THEM STEP AWAY.

I left Marie and drove a half hour north to visit Lars. His wife—we'll call her Clara—was a godly woman, but Lars was an avowed unbeliever. Clara had invited me over a couple of times hoping that I might persuade Lars to trust Christ. He was wary of me but we did all right. He was a truly gifted professional artist and I loved seeing his work.

In the days before I came, Lars had been slipping in and out of consciousness. When he was conscious, he usually wasn't lucid. Nonetheless Clara asked if I would visit him once more and try to talk to him about Christ. I had no idea just how I would go about that, but I went. Lars lay in a hospital bed in the living room. Clara sat anxiously on the sofa while I went to his side. He recognized and greeted me with a wry smile. After a moment of small talk I got down to it. "Lars," I said, "I hear your days are numbered."

"That's what they tell me," he said.

"Can I ask you, Lars, are you prepared to meet God?"

His reply caught me completely off guard. "During the

Enlightenment," he began, "many people rejected belief in God."

The Enlightenment!?" I thought. *Yesterday he didn't know where he was and today he's talking to me about the* Enlightenment? Lars proceeded to give me a short philosophy lesson, the unspoken point being, "No, I still do not believe in Christ. And that's that." I asked if I could pray for him and he politely agreed. Then I said good-bye and left. He died a day or two later.

Pastors walk people to the edge of the world and watch them step away. With unbelievers, I feel a kind of dull thud. There is no grace left. God offered extravagant, measureless, priceless grace and they would have none of it. When believers step away, I feel wonder and a little bit of envy.

PRACTICAL DOCTRINE

Pastors grace God's people with the stories of what is yet to come. We keep their chins up looking for Christ's return. In this clinging and cloying world we urge them not to put down their roots. I imagine a pastor being like an elderly uncle of refugee children. He often gathers them to himself and tells them stories of the homeland they have never seen. He tells them that the day they go home they will be a beautiful bride coming down the aisle of the skies to meet her Bridegroom. The homeless children listen wide-eyed as he tells them that their homeland is a kingdom bright and righteous, where life runs in the rivers and grows on trees. "Our King is the King of all kings," says the uncle. "He rides a mighty charger and the armies of heaven follow Him. He knows your name and He is waiting to be with *you*." The uncle tells these stories again and again because, if he doesn't, the children will forget who they are and put down their stakes in Babylon. The challenge isn't how to get them home. The King will take care of that. The uncle's challenge is that he cannot let the King's children forget their home.

One of the curious pastoral challenges in orienting people to thoughts of heaven is that they aren't all that interested in the details. I asked some seminary students what they thought about heaven. One replied candidly, "I don't think much about heaven. I don't think much about mortality." Meaning, I guess, that unless mortality starts to take your breath away, thoughts of heaven can wait like the defibrillator we have stored in a church cabinet.

Some years ago, after reading Randy Alcorn's book *Heaven*, I decided to preach five sermons from Revelation 21–22, a series I titled, "When God Makes Everything New." When I emailed a good and godly friend that I would be preaching about heaven he wrote back:

> The practical side of me says it does little good to study about heaven. All we can know now is that it will exceed any of our dreams and expectations. It is comforting to talk about at funerals. But people have immediate struggles here on earth that are more effectively addressed by other texts and topics. Having said that, heaven is probably a subject someone like myself should be eager to study, partly so I can have a better attitude. . . . My prayers are with you.

Actually, our "immediate struggles here on earth" are precisely the reason pastors talk about Christ's return and our everlasting life with Him. Heaven is *not* just for funerals, although the promise of heaven turns Christian funerals downside up.

Faith, according to Hebrews 11, is sustained by "looking forward to the city with foundations, whose architect and builder is God." Just ask Father Abraham. We follow in the footsteps of a cloud of witnesses who admitted "that they were aliens and strangers on earth . . . looking for a country of their own . . . longing for a better country—a heavenly one. Therefore God is not ashamed to be called their God, for he has prepared a city for them" (Hebrews 11:10, 13–16). The more we know about that city, the more clear-eyed and tough-minded our faith will be.

SAYING THAT HEAVEN WILL BE WONDERFUL DOESN'T DO IT JUSTICE! THE DELIGHT IS IN THE DETAILS.

Each of the doctrines of our faith is practical and pastoral. Each is necessary for Christians to love and serve Christ. Each is a treasure pastors open to the saints. But I have a soft spot for the doctrine of everlasting life. Sometimes on Friday afternoons, when the week has been harried and an undone sermon weighs heavily, I put on a recording of the song, "No More Night." I lean back, close my eyes, and get homesick as I listen to the words, "No more night. No more pain. No more tears. Never crying again." I weep every time I hear it, and then I'm ready to go back to work. So far as I know, I'm not dying any more than you are. But the thought of heaven sustains me. That's the way it should be.

ALL WE KNOW

In a recent sermon on 1 Corinthians 13, I spent a few moments on the full knowledge, maturity, and clarity Christians will enjoy in heaven. After the service a visitor said sweetly, "All we really know about heaven is that it will be wonderful."

"Actually," I said, "that's not true. We know a lot more than that." I learned later that this woman is not a believer, but a lot of the Christians we shepherd think the same thing.

To begin with, Christians use the word *heaven* as a kind of catchall for different stages of our glorious hope: for the paradise where saints wait now for Christ to return, for the millennial kingdom of Christ, and for that endless era of the "new heavens and the new earth" when "the old order of things has passed away," and God Himself will be with us to wipe every tear from our eyes. Each of these phases is precious. Each helps us persevere.

There is no shortage of detail in the Bible. A pastor can take people to peer through the open door set before John in Revelation 4 and 5 to see the jeweled colors and fantastic beings of the throne room of the Lord God Almighty and the

Lamb. Revelation is full of heaven's hymns, each with a context and story. You can mine every line of Revelation 21 and 22 for details of the New Jerusalem. The sight is astounding. Ponder Jesus' promise to come again for us in John 14:1–4. Look carefully at all we are told about our new bodies in 1 Corinthians 15:35–57. Jesus gives us glimpses of heaven in some of His parables, like the story of the good and faithful servant or the unsettling story of the rich man and Lazarus. And don't forget about the stirring details of Jesus' second coming in 1 Thessalonians 4:13–18 and in Jesus' own descriptions of His return in the Gospels. Saying that heaven will be wonderful doesn't do it justice! The delight is in the details.

ONE OF MY FAVORITE PASTORAL DUTIES
IS TO MAKE PEOPLE HOMESICK.

There is no sense in Scripture that any of these passages were set apart only for the dying or for Christian funerals. Paul's description of Christ's second coming concludes, "Therefore, encourage each other with these words." His extraordinary description of our resurrection bodies in 1 Corinthians 15 comes to the pastoral point in verse 58: "Stand firm. Let nothing move you. Always give yourselves fully to the work of the Lord, because you know that your labor in the Lord is not in vain." These passages are rallying cries for the army of the King: "Onward Christian soldiers!"

MAKE THEM HOMESICK

God gives His people a homing instinct when the Holy Spirit comes to dwell within us. It is a little like having a forward memory. I'm not saying we remember being in heaven before we were born. We weren't. But it is *like* that. In his essay "The Weight of Glory," C. S. Lewis wrote:

> Our lifelong nostalgia, our longing to be reunited with something in the universe from which we now feel cut off, to be on the inside of some door which we have always seen from the outside, is no mere neurotic fancy, but the truest index of our real situation. And to be at last summoned inside would be both glory and honour beyond all our merits and also the healing of that old ache.[3]

One of my favorite pastoral duties is to make people homesick. Remember the Israelites' faithless yammering about going back to Egypt? We can't let that happen in our churches. Whether in worship services or conversations, here are some ways to make people homesick.

Dwell on the details till imagination kicks in. Take any of the texts I've just mentioned above and focus on one or two details until you break through the crust of overfamiliarity. I was preparing to preach about the new heavens and the new earth. I wanted to help people see that we will live in a real creation not so different from our own. At the time I happened to be reading the Pulitzer Prize winning novel *Gilead* by Marilynne Robinson, a Christian. One reason I love that book is because it is about two old pastors. In my sermon I read what one of them tells us about his friend:

> Boughton says he has more ideas about heaven every day. He said, "Mainly I just think about the splendors of the world and multiply by two. I'd multiply by ten or twelve if I had the energy. But two is much more than sufficient for my purposes." So he's sitting there multiplying the feel of the wind by two, multiplying the smell of the grass by two.[4]

We have to be careful not to let our imaginations take us where Scripture has not cut a trail. But Robinson's biblical imagination helped me open the saints' eyes to the new creation God has promised.

For another sermon I meditated on what a *holy* city will be like. Every face is the face of a friend, and every friend is strikingly like Jesus. All the infinitely varied ways "his servants will serve him" will be like a complicated, layered anthem in many parts, a Hallelujah Chorus of activity. Imagine a vast yet intimate fellowship in which God Himself illumines all we do, where all the variety of every culture is brought into our life with Him, and where the likes of us reign—*reign*—forever and ever.

Pastors, we haven't done our work if we only exegete phrases and do word studies. We must let the Spirit shape our imaginations of heaven through the specific details of Scripture, and then we tell God's people till they get a faraway look in their eyes.

Tell stories of the saints' hopes and homegoings. One

Sunday I told my flock about Polycarp, the aged disciple of John who was burned at the stake in AD 155 When the Roman proconsul begged him to recant his faith and save his life Polycarp responded, "Eighty-six years I have served Christ, and He never did me any wrong. How can I blaspheme my King who saved me?"

I've told about my own father, Lyle, who died suddenly at age sixty-three. He was shaving for church when he collapsed. I learned that the Sunday before, the person who was scheduled to bring the special music in our little country church had to cancel and Dad agreed to fill in at the last minute. He sang, "It will be worth it all when we see Jesus. Life's trials will seem so small when we see Christ." Somewhere in the middle of the song he uncharacteristically choked up and began to weep. Marge at the piano finished singing it for him. It was the last time he was ever in church. One week later he was with Jesus.

Every congregation has stories of the hope of heaven—of Christians who have endured for heaven's sake and funerals alive with assurance. Annie brought Brenda, her friend from work, to see me. Brenda had recently attended a Christian funeral in an African-American church. The celebration of hope that she saw there—the singing and joy—literally terrified her. She could not imagine how people could react that way to a death. She ran from the grave, you might say, bewildered and afraid. When I told her that Christians lose their fear of death and hell because of our faith in Christ, that's all she needed to hear. She received Christ right there on the spot and went home rejoicing.

Worship and sing! Songs about Christ's return and heaven make people homesick. We devote two or three worship services a year to those themes. Surely God deserves our praise for such a hope! It is surprising how hard it is to find fresh songs for these services, so we tap into various styles. Not long ago in a service celebrating our hope of Christ's return we sang the spiritual, "In that Great Gettin' Up Morning," the southern gospel classic, "I'll Fly Away," the hymn, "Crown Him with Many Crowns," and the newer worship song, "Crown Him King of Kings." You may have to look for newer songs about heaven, but you do your congregation a favor when you teach them to the church. Just like soldiers far from home, Christians need to sing of heaven, lest we lose heart in the battle.

I don't know if other people have a favorite word, but mine is *home*. I lead a service at a retirement community every month. I told them recently, "I don't preach so often about heaven because you're old. I do it because I'm homesick." That's why I love a Michael Card song I sometimes use as a benediction there as well as at church. The first verse ends, "In this fearful, fallen place, I will *be* your home." And the second verse, about God's summons, ends, "*From* this fearful, fallen place, I will *bring* you home."

Not long ago I visited Belle in the hospital. She is ninety-five. I first met her when she came to the retirement community service. The Thursday evening I preached about the shepherd seeking the one lost sheep, Belle wept through most of it. I think that was the night Jesus carried her back to the flock from the wilds. When I visited her hospital room I made sure she was trusting Christ and then I sang some old hymns. "Sing the one about home," she said. So I did, a true benediction, and she mouthed all the words along with me till we got to the end, "I will bring you . . . home."

"LEAD ME GENTLY HOME"

I read an article in the paper recently about a woman who is a certified birth doula—a midwife—but she also helps people "pass on." She is brought in "to make the environment as peaceful as possible for the person who is dying as well as for family members and friends." The writer said, "That makes her a death doula, a death midwife." Pastors are kind of like that for the people of God. We help when they are born of the Spirit, and we help when they fall asleep in Jesus.

Death does not always come slowly, nor to those who have lived long. Pastors know that only too well. But when I see death coming, I always pray the line from another old song, "Lead her gently home, Father."

When I was a young pastor, I didn't know what to say to people who were dying. I was afraid of sounding morbid. Now I ask direct questions. "Do you think about heaven very much these days?" I might ask. "Are you afraid of what is ahead?" "Do you think much about Jesus?" I think people appreciate someone to talk with about these things.

Like most pastors, I read the Bible to them and assure them that God has put His angels in charge of them to keep them in all their ways. I often need to assure them that their family will be all right and that they can let go. I hold their hands and kiss them on the forehead when I leave.

When death comes, I am always gripped by the mystery. When Jim died, the gracious candy man I told you about, I reached the hospital before anyone in his family. Ten minutes sooner and I could have said good-bye. I stepped into his dark room alone. A nurse had just left and the sheet was pulled neatly up to his chin. He was gone, of course. The mystery almost took my breath away. What had just happened? What were those moments like for Jim? Just how does Jesus welcome home His beloved?

ONE CLAP

The Puritan Thomas Brooks wrote, "Remember, all other preparations are to no purpose, if a man is not prepared to die. . . . As death leaves you—so judgment shall find you! As the judgment finds you—so shall eternity keep you!"

On the afternoon of May 2, 1990, I heard holy things. I visited a father and husband named Larry. He was just in his thirties and near death from cancer. I had gone to serve him Communion because he was too weak to come to church. He was a deeply thoughtful man, and that day as he spoke slowly and deliberately, I realized I was hearing extraordinary things. I started scribbling them in a bulletin I found in my Bible.

"Even if I have a short time to live," Larry said, "He's given me a great hope. Sometimes life throws us some tremendous curves, but death has lost its sting."

I wrote up and down the margins of that bulletin as Larry talked about suffering, about his struggle for faith, and his experience of God's strength. "At the point in my life when I'm the weakest," he said, "I'm the strongest I've ever been."

We started talking about his funeral, which, as it turned out, would be exactly one month later. He told me he wanted lots of singing. I remembered how Larry would put his head back and sing with unabashed gusto. I asked him what he wanted his funeral to be like. He said, "The only thing I want people to think on that day is joy; is . . ." and he raised his hands deliberately and then clapped once, slowly and grandly. "When I pass into His kingdom I envision this spectacular light, this spectacular feeling of being able to let go. I've felt a lot of grief for my children, my wife, my family, myself, but I've had to get over that. But once you get past that, you know that God is there—that spirit of joyfulness."

"It's going to be a happy day for me," Larry said, grace thick in the room. "No grief for me. God chose me this time!"

Chapter Eleven

"SAFE THUS FAR"

THE WEEKEND I candidated for the church I now serve, I went to an early Friday morning men's prayer meeting. It was still dark outside as we grabbed cups of coffee and sweet rolls and sat in the circle of chairs. I was introduced as the pastoral candidate, but Clyde came in late and he had no idea who I was. He took the empty chair next to me. I asked his name and what he did. He said he was a consultant working in executive placement. Then, to my surprise, he asked me what I did. He didn't know. Opportunity knocked!

"I'm a shepherd," I said.

"No kidding!" he exclaimed, taken aback. "Shepherd. I know there used to be a pig farm around here." (It isn't easy to find common ground with a shepherd.) "How big is your, ah, farm?" he asked. "How many sheep do you have?"

"It's pretty good-sized," I said. "I have several hundred sheep."

"How interesting!" Clyde said, still flailing. "Where do you send them for shearing?"

I broke it to him. "Actually, I'm a spiritual shepherd," I said. "A pastor. Your church is considering calling me."

It is difficult for people to understand pastors. Once I was talking with a sales manager of a hotel when he asked, "So what do you do?"

Like other pastors, I know that the answer to that question usually makes people pull back, as guarded as if you told them you worked for the IRS. But I told him, "I'm a pastor."

"Really," he said, mentally scrambling to get his footing. "You don't look like a pastor."

I took that as a compliment.

IT IS AMAZING WHAT SACRED THINGS
WE HANDLE AND WHAT HOLY PEOPLE WE LEAD.

I guess secular people don't really have a category for those of us who handle holy tasks. They get skittish around people who have devoted their careers to serving God and who talk to Him out loud in public. We're the only people they have ever met who can legally say, "I pronounce you husband and wife" on one occasion and on another, "Dust to dust, ashes to ashes." And they don't know the half of it.

Our work really is unique, a mystery even. Pastors are Christ's Wordworkers. We are in the practice of grace. The people we serve are the flock of God and Jesus has drafted us out from among them to be their shepherds. We know what they often forget—that they are saints, "the church of the firstborn," according to Hebrews; "everlasting splendours," as C. S. Lewis put it. For such an earthy job as shepherding, it is amazing what sacred things we handle and what holy people we lead. It is a wonder that our hands and hearts aren't singed.

GRACE GREENHOUSE

I've entered my sixties. I can see more clearly now what John Newton meant: "'Tis grace hath brought me safe thus far, and grace will lead me home." Being a pastor puts us in a kind of grace greenhouse. We deal in grace more than most people. We study and proclaim its Christ-rooted intricate beauty from Scripture. We see it up close in the lives of the saints. We draw upon grace constantly to do the unique work we're called to do. I would not say I know more of grace than other Christians, but I think it is safe to say that I know more of grace than I would have if I had not been a pastor.

I have come to appreciate how relentless God's grace is. God really does hound people with His love, especially when someone is praying for them. That's why pastors are in such a good position. We settle in with a group of God's people for years and let the grace inherent in godly shepherding just plug away.

Pastors often do very ordinary things that God infuses with His grace. God can time our note or phone call so that, unknown to us, it arrives like a miracle. We talk to someone about taking on a ministry or about something they need to straighten out, only to find that God has them ready and waiting. I think sometimes they must wonder if we're clairvoyant, but it is just the timing of God's grace.

GRACE OCCASIONALLY WORKS
IN A BURST OF GLORY, BUT MOST
OF THE TIME IT IS AS SLOW AS SUMMER.

Pastors go into the ministry hoping to see lives changed through Christ. And we do. But like the clock on my wall says, "Things take time." Take preaching, for example. Twice now, in two different churches, I have preached well over five hundred sermons. I don't know if any single one of those sermons was life changing for someone, but I am certain that the accumulated effect of many sermons sanctifies people. I heard somewhere that tug boats move huge ships by bumping them. Bump. Bump. Bump. And slowly the great vessel turns. Preaching, and all pastoring, is like that. We bump lives with pastoral graces—sermons, services, meals, conversations, touches of kindness and discipline, even our waiting—and over time we help people become more like Jesus. Miraculously, we become more like Him in the process as well. Grace occasionally works in a burst of glory, but most of the time it is as slow as summer.

IS MY FATHER EVER PROUD OF ME?

For many years I wondered if my heavenly Father was ever proud of me. I believed, true to the gospel, that He loved me regardless of what I had done wrong. But what did He think of the things I had done *well*? Was God ever proud of a sermon I had preached? If I sacrificed to care for someone in church, would He see and smile as if to say, "That's My boy"?

I suspected that I was hoping for too much. I assumed my best efforts were only what He expected. I was only doing what a servant should do. After all, "From everyone who has been given much, much will be demanded." And I know I have been given much.

Gradually, over several months, the Holy Spirit helped me sort this out. Of course God is proud of me when I serve Him well! He is a *Father*! I remember reading Brennan Manning's story of Seamus, the eighty-year-old Irishman skipping along the shores of Lake Killarney as the sun rose on his birthday. When his nephew asked why he was skipping, he said, "You see, the Father is fond of me. Ah, me Father is so very fond of me." The story literally took my breath away. What hadn't been clear became obvious: if my Father is fond of me, then surely He delights to see me do my best. Gradually I came to sense the pleasure of God when I pastored well. It was a great relief and very liberating.

Yet there is this caveat: "The Lord looks at the heart." God only delights in our work when it is shaped by three good-hearted qualities: faith, love, and hope. Paul says in the opening lines of 1 Thessalonians, "We continually remember before our God and Father your work produced by *faith*, your labor prompted by *love*, and your endurance inspired by *hope* in our Lord Jesus Christ."

"Work produced by faith." Nothing worthwhile is built without faith in Christ as Savior and without commitment to *the* faith as set forth in Scripture. Faith in Christ as Savior comes easy to me. Faith in the cardinal doctrines poses no difficulty. Where faith gets hard for me is in everyday pastoral work. For example, it takes faith not to panic early on Sunday morning when my sermon lies limp and panting on a page. It takes faith to believe I can go home at night without a full briefcase or take my day off, even though the Lord's work mounts up behind me. It takes faith to believe God will give me the words to say in a situation I cannot script. It takes faith to let God work through a board or congregation without my manipulation.

For years I have been learning in the daily duties of the ministry to stop and pray, and then to lean back on the hand of God in my back to see if I'm going in the right direction. I wait for His nudge. "Lord, should I go visit or stay here and study?" "Am I on the right track with this exegesis or am I missing something?" "Is this ministry idea right for us now or should I wait?" I pray and consider. I think of the phrase used by the Jerusalem Council in Acts 15:28, "It seemed good to the Holy Spirit and to us. . . ." When I can say that, I proceed in faith.

Now when I can look at a sermon, a counseling session, or the plans we're developing for a ministry, and know that I exercised the muscles of faith—that I consciously trusted God with the decision making and the work—then I know that my Father is pleased.

"Labor prompted by love." Unfortunately, love does not always prompt a pastor's labor. For example, I see now that I have worked very hard sometimes because I was afraid. I worked frantically so that no one would have reason to criticize. I would put on niceness like David trying on Saul's worthless armor. I would politick desperately to manage stubborn members because I was so afraid of the possible mess.

Other times my labor may have only been prompted by sheer creative energy. I've immersed myself in some great program because the artist in me wanted a big canvas. People usually loved it. But I'm not sure now how much I was loving them, so I don't know what good it did.

Then there has been the grueling labor driven by pastoral peer pressure. There are trends that sweep the pastoral world from time to time that seem to reset everyone's agenda. Sometimes they are invigorating for ministry, but not always. The one that nearly did me in was the growing emphasis in the mid 1980s for pastors to be visionary. It seemed like everywhere I turned other pastors were talking about vision. I had never heard that language before and it seemed that suddenly it was the very measure of our work. That terrible KJV translation of Proverbs 29:18, "Where there is no vision, the people perish," became a cruel taskmaster that I could not satisfy. I became depressed. Those months were the only time in more than thirty-five years when I seriously thought I might need to leave the ministry. After all, I apparently didn't have "a vision," and the hours we leaders spent dutifully writing one was a loveless, crushing duty to me. I didn't know then that shepherding the flock of God can birth vision naturally. No one told me that pastoral vision doesn't necessarily require a statement that fits on a sign over the door. I hadn't learned yet that love takes the feel of chrome and plastic out of vision statements and helps us not only lead a congregation into the future but also to lead them on paths of righteousness for His name's sake.

THE CHURCH NEEDS OLD
SHEPHERDS, SO I STAND READY.

I love the church I serve. I really love them. I love them when I preach, go to meetings, field phone calls, and organize programs. I love to see their faces and I enjoy their company. I love what the Lord Jesus is perfecting in them. So, when that is true, God is pleased with my work.

"Endurance inspired by hope in our Lord Jesus Christ." Each year at our denomination's annual conference there is a luncheon for our ministerial association. Each year a dozen or two pastors who have reached sixty-five years are recognized as lifetime members. I remember looking at those men when I was young. I would imagine all the sermons they had preached, all the meetings they had attended, and all the stresses they had faced for the Lord's sake. To me they were like veterans I'd see marching in the Fourth of July parade. I was proud to be in their company and proud to be a recruit.

Now that day is not far away for me. Soon I can be a "lifetime member" of the ministerial association and won't have to pay dues any more. However I am not ready yet to talk retirement, even though I can't keep up the pace I once did. The church needs old shepherds, so I stand ready. Someday, of course, the time will come to turn in my keys. I want more than anything to meet that day as an honorable shepherd who leaves behind churches who know the grace of our Lord Jesus Christ.

It isn't necessarily harder for pastors to endure in the faith than other believers; but there is often more at stake should we fail, and I do think that we are especially vulnerable. Pastoral endurance requires being vigilant in guarding our own souls, as well as dogged faithfulness to Christ, the calling He has given us, and the people He died to redeem. Still, no matter how determined we are, who of us would still be standing at the end were it not for God's mercy and strength?

When I was in my midthirties I witnessed some dear brothers lose their ministries because of sin. Thankfully, they did not fall from grace, but they could no longer shepherd the flock of God. First, I was sad. Then, frightened. And finally, fatalistic. It was the other time in my life that I thought of Pickett's Charge, that doomed debacle at the Battle of Gettysburg where so many soldiers were mowed down. I looked at my fallen pastoral brothers, men as good and called as I, and I began to think, *It is only a matter of time. My sin will be the death of me, too. I may get a few steps farther, but it seems like we will all go down.* It was a desperate feeling for a young pastor.

Then, by the grace of God, I came across Jude 24, "To him who is able to keep you from falling and to present you before his glorious presence without fault and with great joy." I have clung to that verse for more than twenty-five years. I am no less a danger to myself now than I was then, but that makes the verse all the more precious. He is *still* able to keep me from falling. He is *still* able to present me to the Father without fault and with great joy. How that can possibly be, I do not know, except for grace. "'Tis *grace* hath brought me safe thus far."

THE CHIEF SHEPHERD AND THE CROWN

Peter was Christ's first under-shepherd. It was after his dismal denial of Jesus that the Lord spoke to him on the beach and said, "Feed my lambs. . . . Take care of my sheep. . . . Feed my sheep." And having fallen flat on his face and been raised by grace, he became the first pastor. It has been a grace job from the very beginning. That makes his charge in 1 Peter 5:1–4 worth reading again:

> To the elders among you, I appeal as a fellow elder, a wit-
> ness of Christ's sufferings and one who also will share in the
> glory to be revealed: Be shepherds of God's flock that is
> under your care, serving as overseers—not because you
> must, but because you are willing, as God wants you to be;

not greedy for money, but eager to serve; not lording it over those entrusted to you, but being examples to the flock. And when the Chief Shepherd appears, you will receive the crown of glory that will never fade away.

Here is a great Christian promise personalized for the church's shepherds. Our coming King wears many crowns and is worthy of many exalted names, but perhaps what is dearest to us is that He is a shepherd like us. He is our "Chief Shepherd," our beloved Senior Pastor with whom we have worked all these years. He knows what it is like to shepherd the flock of God.

I know this is kind of a silly picture, but imagine us all gathered in heaven, thrilled to finally be together with all our brothers and sisters in the Lord. Then someone says, "Let's get a picture of all the shepherds here." Some agreeably begin to bunch together, the tall ones pushing the short ones forward. And then Jesus comes to us. "I want to be in this picture," He says. "Shepherds are My kind of people." So we proudly scrunch in close around Him—all who have borne this calling over the centuries—all those plain, ordinary, unremarkable folks who have shepherded equally ordinary flocks. And I imagine Him pointing at me and saying, "Come on, Lee . . . You are one of My shepherds! I want you in this picture with Me."

Pastors are also promised, "You will receive the crown of glory that will never fade away." Shepherds don't usually wear crowns. But then there was King David and King Jesus, shepherd kings. All believers will be given crowns in heaven—signals of our reigning with Christ. I hope ours has a little shepherd's staff logo on it or something. Revelation 7:17 says,

"For the Lamb at the center of the throne *will be their shepherd*; he will lead them to springs of living water. And God will wipe away every tear from their eyes." If Jesus remains our Chief Shepherd forever, I wonder if somehow we might continue to shepherd with Him.

Peter's promise of the Chief Shepherd's return assures us that pastors will not be forgotten in some lonely pasture. One day the bleating of sheep will be drowned out in the trumpet call of God. One day we will leave our last committee meeting to find ourselves in the company of angels. One day we will make our last hospital call or officiate at our last funeral and be ushered into that Kingdom where there is no more death or mourning or crying or pain. One day we will put aside our monthly reports and Sunday bulletins to take up the endless anthems of glory. One day we will preach our last sermons and lay aside our beloved Bibles to find ourselves awestruck in the presence of Him whose very name is the Word of God. One day we will set aside the cups and bread for the last time in order to take our places at the wedding supper of the Lamb. And when that day comes, we will lay down our staffs and take our rest, for the sheep we have fed and led and guarded will be safe at last in the fold of Jesus. Then we will hear, "Well done!" from the Chief Shepherd whose lambs we have loved.

ALL THE TRUMPETS

In John Bunyan's *The Pilgrim's Progress, Part 2,* Christian's wife, Christiana, along with their children, make their way to the Celestial City. They come upon "a man with his sword drawn, and his face all bloody, who tells them, 'I am one whose name is VALIANT-FOR-TRUTH. I am a pilgrim, and am going to the Celestial City.'" He becomes their rear guard lest "some fiend, or dragon, or giant, or thief, should fall upon [them], and so do mischief."

I want to be like that man. A pastor, Mr. Valiant-for-Truth, the guardian of God's homeward bound pilgrims, the sword of God's Word in my hand. My favorite lines in all of literature describe what happens as this pilgrim band nears the Celestial City and this guardian hero is called home.

> After this it was noised abroad that Mr. VALIANT-FOR-TRUTH was sent for by a summons. . . . When he understood it, he called for his friends, and told them of it. Then said he, "I am going to my Father's house: and though with great difficulty I have got hither, yet now I do not repent me of all the troubles I have been at to arrive where I am. My sword I give to him that shall succeed me in my pilgrimage, and my courage and skill to him that can get it. My marks and scars I carry with me, to be a witness for me that I have fought his battles, who will now be my rewarder." When the day that he must go home was come, many accompanied him to the river-side, into which, as he went down, he said, "O death where is thy sting?" And as he went down deeper, he cried, "O grave, where is thy victory?" So he passed over, and all the trumpets sounded for him on the other side.[5]

By the grace of God, let us shepherd the flock of God faithfully and bravely until all the trumpets sound for us on the other side.

NOTES

1. Quoted in Philip Yancey, *What's So Amazing About Grace?* (Grand Rapids: Zondervan, 1997), 32.

2. Frederick Buechner, *On the Road with the Archangel* (New York: HarperCollins, 1997), 1.

3. C. S. Lewis, *The Weight of Glory and Other Addresses* (New York: the Macmillan Company, 1949), 12.

4. Marilynne Robinson, *Gilead* (New York: Farrar, Straus and Giroux, 2004), 147.

5. John Bunyan, *The Pilgrim's Progress, The Second Part* (Uhrichsville, OH: Barbour Books, 1985), 376.

ACKNOWLEDGMENTS

MY PARENTS, Lyle and Grace, made church a natural part of life. As the psalmist said, "You have given me the heritage of those who fear your name" (Psalm 61:5).

I am the product of other pastors—too many to mention—but I think so often of two. Pastor Don Johanson came to our little rural church fresh out of seminary and loved us junior-high kids for all he was worth. Pastor Wayne Lehsten was the senior pastor who welcomed me to his staff after God called me to ministry. It was with him that I learned to love being a pastor.

Three churches welcomed me as their shepherd and loved me and my family well: North Suburban Evangelical Free Church (Deerfield, Illinois); Chippewa Evangelical Free Church (Beaver Falls, Pennsylvania); and the Village Church of Lincolnshire (Lake Forest, Illinois). To quote *Law & Order*, "these are their stories."

Craig Brian Larson, editor of *Preaching Today*, gave me the opportunity to write about preaching, which opened the door for me to write for you.